RUTH
LEAVES
HOME

ALTHEA GREENIDGE

WESTBOW
PRESS®
A DIVISION OF THOMAS NELSON
& ZONDERVAN

WestBow Press books may be ordered through booksellers or by contacting:

WestBow Press
A Division of Thomas Nelson & Zondervan
1663 Liberty Drive
Bloomington, IN 47403
www.westbowpress.com
1 (866) 928-1240

ISBN: 978-1-5127-6753-7 (sc)

Print information available on the last page.

WestBow Press rev. date: 03/03/2017

TABLE OF CONTENTS

PREFACE

Young adults are fascinating and ever so vulnerable. Being a secondary teacher of long standing, I have had first hand opportunities to influence young lives in a somewhat limited manner regarding the pithy issues of life; I say 'limited' because being a language teacher, and not a counsellor, there is a limit to what I can say to steer them in the right direction on life matters during language classes.

I have been able, on a few occasions, during PSHE, and whole-day workshops, to plant seeds about healthy relationships between young men and women, in an attempt to shatter the negative models to which they are exposed in the media.

It is my sincere hope that some seeds fell on fertile, receptive ground.

Ruth leaves home was also written in an attempt to show the importance of a solid home foundation, -train up a child in the way he should go, and when he is old he will not depart from it (Proverbs 22:6). Additionally, it was written to demonstrate the all-embracing love of God, who welcomes His children back with loving arms even after they left and went away to a far country (a life of sin and unrighteous living).

INTRODUCTION

What happens when three friends decide to room together for university, never having encountered certain of life's challenges before? *Ruth leaves home* is a story about decisions- some good, some poor, that Ruth, Shanice and Lizzy make in an attempt to assert themselves as independent young adults.

While the idea seems like a good one on the surface, as the story unfolds, the reader sees that the ravages of life soon begin to overcome the girls. The book is not an 'I told you so' narrative, which is supposed to act as a scare tactic to choose God and His way, but it presents many true life experiences that the author experienced when living without the covering of divine protection.

Ruth, the protagonist, is saved, and represents the moral sounding board who keeps the friendships held together, but she herself is not devoid of certain challenges in the workplace. She depends largely on the advice of a family friend, Aunt Ellen whom she invites to the flat to speak to her friends about relationships and matters of intimacy between men and women.

Shanice is a vivacious, opinionated, popular young woman who thinks that she has all the answers, yet finds herself almost duped into working at an escort agency. She is so trusting, and so blinded by external appearances that she is drawn into a friendship group with a bunch of worldly, flashy, materialistic girls, one of whom ends up pregnant for one of her clients at the escort agency.

Lizzy is the most vulnerable of the three. Sweet, naive and innocent, she comes from a family in which her parents divorced after living as married cohabiters because her father fell out of love with her mother. All Lizzy ever wanted was to be loved by her father, and as a result, she ends up in a relationship with a married university professor who senses her vulnerability and impresses her with his sophistication. Things came to a crashing halt for her when she ended up stranded in the toilet of a sex club that she was taken to by the professor.

CHAPTER 1

RUTH LEAVES HOME

¹⁷ And I have promised to bring you up out of your misery in Egypt into the land of the Canaanites, Hittites, Amorites, Perizzites, Hivites and Jebusites—a land flowing with milk and honey.' Ex 3:17 (NIV)

"I wish I could get this Scripture out of my head," Ruth thought, exasperated. All day it had been resonating in her mind, and she had no time to think of any such thing, especially now that she had finally decided to leave home, and tell her parents about it. She had mentioned it to them earlier on that day at breakfast, and she could tell by the look on her father's face that dinner would be a challenge. She even thought of stopping off and eating at the local fast food restaurant, but decided against it; she would still have to go home afterwards anyway, so she might as well have a healthy, and tasty meal at home, amidst the sparks that would possibly be flying.

Ruth was eighteen, and getting ready to go to university. She felt ready to move out on her own –well, it wouldn't really be on her own; she had spoken with two other friends who both had part-time jobs, and together they hatched a plan to find a flat and move in as flatmates. There was only one bedroom, but it was large enough to hold three single beds, and the rent was manageable.

She was apprehensive about breaking the news to her parents but decided that it was the decent thing to do, instead of just leaving when they were at work, and sticking a post-it on the refrigerator for them to find when they returned: that would be cruel, and unkind. She loved them too much to break their hearts like that. She figured that even though there would be arguments, and raised voices, at least she would be going about it in a mature manner.

As far as she was concerned, her parents were both too protective, and a bit old-fashioned. They thought that she should stay at home until she was about to get married, or at least when she had completed all her studies, and had settled into the career of her choice. If she decided to do that she envisaged being at home at least until she was twenty-seven! She loved her parents, but couldn't bear the thought of living under their watchful eyes until she was that old. Goodness, how could she possibly meet any interesting people, and try being independent enough to finally settle down with someone if all she heard was what the Bible said. Mind you, she was a regular church-goer, and believed in God, but she knew in her heart that she could never win an argument when she was up against the word of God! She had considered going to university in another city, or even another country to escape their watchful gaze, and prove to them that she was capable of succeeding without their approval on every matter, but her close friends Elizabeth and Shanice were staying in London, and she wanted to be with them, seeing that they had been friends since primary school.

Ruth had quite a few decisions to make regarding her new life, and the biggest one that was weighing on her mind was whether she would continue attending church, that is, the same church that she had attended for the past eighteen years. She had grown up in that church, and really enjoyed it. There were times in secondary school when her friends teased her about being a born again Christian, and not being allowed to go to parties, or even spend the night at friends' houses. She always laughed it off with them, but began feeling slightly differently about her life when she attended a seminar in college on women as free thinkers in the modern world. A few of the concepts presented clashed with what she had been taught at church, and at home, but she did not see the harm in expressing herself as a free thinker alongside her Bible foundation. She felt personally convicted that she was responsible enough to have a successful life, making decisions on her own. As a matter of fact, her two future flatmates had said that she was the most responsible out of the three, and they felt that she was the one who could be trusted to make major decisions; she would have to remember to tell her parents that during their discussion at dinner time.

She took a deep breath as she put the key in the door and turned it. As she entered the hallway and began taking off her jumper, the smell of her mother's cooking wafted towards her. It smelled better than she could ever remember, and she began to feel nostalgic about it even though she had not yet moved out: she was going to miss mother's great cooking, but she was grateful that she had learned to make most of the dishes she enjoyed. She secretly wished that she could still come home for meals though.

She entered the kitchen and hugged her mum from the back and kissed her on the cheek. Her mother turned towards her and smiled. She looked sad. She took Ruth's face in her hands and kissed her on the forehead. Ruth loved it when she did that, it made her feel like a little girl again: very reassured and comforted. She stifled back the tears and went into the living room to say hello to her father. She felt strangely brave. Telling them that she was moving out was the hardest thing, and since that hurdle was over, she would just have to steel herself for whatever arguments and counter arguments they would try to present to her to convince her not to leave.

"Hello dad." She said as she bent to kiss him.

"Ruth. I didn't hear you come in. Hello. How was your day?"

What? Did she hear right? No mention of her decision to leave home? Was she awake?

"It was ok. I got an email from the bank saying they approved the loan. I can save Nan's money, and use it in case of an emergency, and to help buy a few things for the flat." Should she have brought that up so soon? What was she doing? She had everything all planned out, and now she was not going according to script. What was wrong with her?

"What a blessing. Did you tell mum?"

3

"No. I was going to wait until dinner, but I got excited and blurted it out to you." She was more perplexed than excited. Her father seemed very calm, and this was unnerving her. According to the script that she had in her head, things weren't supposed to be going so smoothly. Oh well, there was still dinner to come, but she couldn't see things turning out that bad if they had begun so well.

She left the room and went to take a shower before dinner. Actually, she just wanted to think. The reaction of her father had really thrown her. He wasn't a tyrant or anything like that, but when he felt really strongly about a matter he let it permeate through every action, and conversation. So far, he hadn't said a single word about her moving out. She could see that her mum looked sad, and reasoned that her decision to leave was the cause of it, but her dad...huh! She honestly didn't know what to make of his behaviour.

She decided to call Shanice and tell her.

"Hey girl! You still alive? I was sure you'd be floating down the Thames River by now. How is it going over there?"

"You would never believe how calm they are. I can tell that mum's been crying, but dad...man, he seems so cool. I don't know what to think?"

"What? For real? Girl if I were you, I would leave that house. That does not sound natural. Pack your things and leave before they turn on you."

"I'm too hungry for that. And I've used up even more energy freaking out about why they are acting so normal. Lemme go. I'll call you later and tell you how it went down."

"Later."

She took a quick shower and went downstairs.

"Where are Hannah and Jonathan? Do they have extra classes this evening?" She asked her mother.

"No. They are spending the night at Aunty Ellen's."

Ruth froze. She began to feel cold. Her throat felt dry, really dry. Her parents had sent her brother and sister to spend the night at her aunt's house on a Thursday night. Oh dear. Maybe things were going to turn out bad after all. She had to go into the washroom and drink a little water. She sat on the toilet and took a few deep breaths. She didn't feel so secure after all. After what seemed like a lifetime, but it was only after two minutes, her mum called her to dinner. She tried to compose herself and went into the dining room.

"You all right Ruth?" Her father asked.

"Yes dad. I'm ok."

"Would you like to say a prayer before we eat, then?" He asked.

Say a prayer? She could barely think. She had to appear calm no matter what.

"Erm, yeah. Thank you dear God, erm. Thank you Jehovah Shalom. Sorry. Jehovah Jireh for providing this meal. Thank you. Bless the hands that made it. Bless all the families that are sitting down to dinner. Bless all those who have nothing to eat and no place to live. Keep them in your tender care. In Jesus' name. Amen."

"Amen." Her parents echoed.

"This looks great mum. Too bad Hannah and John aren't here to share it. So why did they go to Aunty Ellen's?"

"We thought that we had a lot to discuss, and that maybe for tonight, they didn't need to be a part of any decisions that would be made."

"Oh. I see. So, dad, mum. Well, you know that I am moving out with Elizabeth and Shanice, right."

"That was what you said this morning. When did you begin planning this, Ruth?" Her father asked.

"Well. You know, we had been playing around with the idea of living together for a short while, maybe even taking a holiday together. Then we got to talking about maybe doing it for uni. Before you know it, we had it all planned."

"Where exactly are you planning on living? What do you mean by 'all planned'? You are starting university in another couple of weeks, Ruth. When will you have the time to find a flat?"

Ruth felt a bit uneasy. "We already found a flat dad. It is in south east London. It is really cosy. You would like it mum."

"What? You have a flat already? I am really surprised at this. Who provided the down payment, and whose utility bills did you use as proof of support?"

"Dad please. We used Elizabeth's mother's bills, and we saved up for the down payment. We only needed one month's security deposit and seeing that the rent is only five hundred pounds a month that was not too bad for us."

"Ruth, please don't tell me that you used your grand-mother's gift to you to finance this plan of yours." Her mother said.

"Just a bit of it mother. I only needed about a hundred and fifty pounds of it."

There was a long, silent pause during which none of them said anything. They just sat silently chewing. Ruth expected her father to say how much she had disappointed them, and her mother to start lecturing her about the dangers of young people living alone. At least she expected a verse from the Bible. But nothing... just an interminable silence.

Finally her father broke the silence: "I am sure you know that this is not what we would have wanted for you. You were not brought up like this. We usually discuss things together in this family, so I can't understand why you decided to make such a life-changing decision with two friends. I mean, have you really thought this through? You are about to start university, Ruth. This is the time that you should be as stress-free as possible, without having to bother about the responsibility of having to work to help support yourself. At this stage of your life, a job should be a means of making a bit of money to save a little to buy personal effects, not as a means of major support. How many hours a week will you have to devote to your studies? Will you be able to study full time?"

"Well, I wanted to talk to you about this too. I decided that for the first year of uni I would go part-time, then afterwards, in the second year, I would do full-time study."

All her mother could say was: "Oh Ruth. But this makes no sense at all. What happens if the rent goes up, and you have to work more hours to pay your way? It usually makes more sense to start out taking more credits then if anything, lessen the load towards the end when the courses become harder. Oh Ruth."

Her father got up and walked to the window. After a couple of minutes he returned to the table.

"What about your friends? Are they also going to be studying part-time?"

"Well, their mums said that they are going to help them with the rent, so they won't have to work so many hours."

"Are you saying that they will be full-time students and you will be a part-timer? No wonder they wanted to room with you. This agreement doesn't seem very equitable at all Ruth. Is this how you have things all planned out?"

"Yes. My friends aren't using me, dad. They are my best friends. They wouldn't do that. You like Elizabeth and Shanice don't you?"

"Ruth, this is what I have to say. I do not like what you have said tonight at all. Not one bit. Why are you so willing to give up the comfort and support you have at home to start a life of uncertainty with two friends whose parents seem eager to push them out of the nest? What do you know about living on your own? What happens when the taps freeze over in the middle of winter? What happens if one of you catches the flu and can't go to work, but have to keep paying the bills? The jobs you do don't offer you enough security to keep you if you are off sick for more than a certain amount of time. My daughter, if this is the life you choose for yourself all I can do is to pray for you. It seems as if you have already made up your mind, so even though I would prefer you to stay at home, I cannot tie you to the place where you do not want to be. Mother and I have discussed this at length today, and we want you to know that while our hearts are heavy about your decision, you will always be our child, and we love you, and will never forsake you. We have only one small request: do not take God out of your life. You will need him now more than ever before. You have been brought up knowing what is right from wrong, and following God's word, do not choose to forsake His way at this stage of your life." He kissed her and left the room.

"Mother, I'm sorry. But I really want to prove to you that I can make it on my own. I love you both so much, and I know that you love me too, but mum, I feel that there is no place in this home for exploring other ideas, and I want to have a chance to explore, mum."

"Ruth. I am not sure what sort of ideas you are talking about, but all I can tell you is this: you may think that the world has a lot to offer you, but at the end of the day there is only one way which leads to the truth. When I was a child my mother used to talk about irreparable damage. Now that I am grown up, I know that Jesus' salvation and the blood can heal any wound, so there is no real irreparable damage. But I understand what my mother meant. There is a way that can lead you down to destruction if you travel too far on it. Make sure you don't walk on that path."

"No mum. I won't."

"I hope that you won't have to work on Sundays and that you will still come to church."

Ruth was silent. She thought that it might have been better not to say that she would be working all day on Sunday. But apart from that, she didn't think that the meeting went too badly. She must remember to call Lizzy and Neecie before going to bed.

CHAPTER 2

NEW LIFE, NEW RESPONSIBILITIES

"Not long after that, the younger son got together all he had, set off for a distant country..." Luke 15:13a (NIV)

Ruth could hardly believe that she was no longer living at home with her parents. Several times during the week she had to pinch herself to check that it wasn't a dream. She ended up with a few bruises on her arms and legs, but they were worth it. She made up her mind that everything would work out for the best; she did not want to end up in a position in which mum and dad would have to say "I told you so." She knew that the road ahead would not always be smooth, but she sat down with Lizzy and Neecie and had a chat about dealing with challenges together, and not letting any one person bear the burden on their own, no matter what it was. She also had a private think session with herself about the matter of church. Seeing that she would not be able to attend on Sundays, she would try and make at least one mid-week service, and remember to pray and read the Bible every day. She hoped that she could keep up with this last promise, because she used to find it a bit difficult to keep up with when she lived at home, and attended church regularly.

It was Saturday morning, and the flatmates were sitting together in the living room getting ready to have a meeting. They decided that one policy they wanted to stick to was to have a meeting every Saturday morning after breakfast to discuss matters dealing with the flat, and just to have a general catch-up, seeing that they had different schedules during the week.

A week had passed since Ruth moved out of her parents' house. She didn't have too much to move, so she packed a suitcase and two small boxes into her father's car, and together they drove to her new flat. Mum cooked her favourite meal; as a matter of fact, she prepared enough for the three friends for a week. What a relief! Her mum was a real gem, and she appreciated her for it.

When they arrived at the flat Elizabeth and Shanice were at work. She invited her family in and gave them a tour of the flat. She desperately wanted their approval, and she felt a lot better when her parents said that they liked the place and that it was in a safe neighbourhood; she breathed a sigh of relief. Before leaving, her father gathered them all together to say a prayer: "Dear father God, I come boldly before your throne of grace and ask for your continued blessings and protection over my family. Father God I ask that you give your angels charge over Ruth, Lizzy and Shanice; bless their going out, and their coming in. Draw a hedge of protection around them, and around this flat. I declare that no weapon formed against them shall prosper, and I condemn any tongue that rises against them. Draw them close to you and watch over them. Thank you for hearing me. I give you all the honour and the glory. In Jesus' name. Amen." And with that they all hugged each other, and her family said goodbye to her.

After they left, Ruth sat on her bed and cried. She wasn't sure why she was crying. She imagined that it was an emotional time, and this was just a moment of release. She checked herself to see if she regretted the decision to leave the only home she had known since birth: a warm, loving, safe environment where she felt like a foetus in a womb. Now, sitting on the edge of a strange bed, she didn't feel that safe anymore. Please God, let it just be a passing cloud of sadness. She got up off the bed, turned on the radio, and began to busy herself unpacking her things and putting them away. Soon enough the cloud passed and she felt a surge of happiness.

That was 6 days ago. Now she sat with her friends talking about the week, and having a laugh.

"All right, girls, shall we call our first official meeting to order?" said Elizabeth.

"I'm all for it. I hereby call this meeting to order." chimed in Shanice. They all began to laugh out loud and rolled over each other on the sofa like giggling children.

"Right girlies, let's see. What about if we come up with a list of do's and don'ts for the flat, and our living arrangements? I think that this is really important so that we don't cross any lines, or have any misunderstandings about certain issues. What do you think?" This was Ruth's first contribution, and she felt very mature bringing up the matter.

"Yeah! Let's do that. I like that. I saw a movie once where some friends broke up their friendship over exactly what you just said Ruthie. They never had any clear set of rules about living together, and then they all started getting on each other's nerves, and arguments broke out. In the end, they not only moved out of the flat, but that was also the end of their friendship." Shanice added.

Ruth and Elizabeth looked at each other and smiled. Shanice loved drama and sensationalism; she would keep them entertained, and they were both looking forward to the many stories she would have to share with them, and the excitement having her there would bring.

"So, can we start with cleaning? I say we clean up after ourselves and not let our mess pile up. That way we won't get into arguments about who left things messy and didn't clean up. What's your vote on that?" Ruth said.

Both girls agreed that this was a good idea.

"I say we make a roster for bathroom and kitchen duty. I mean, yeah, we are going to wash up our individual plates and cups, but what about general cleaning when the flat gets dusty, and the bath needs scrubbing?" Elizabeth wanted to know.

"That is a really good idea. I don't mind doing the kitchen. Should we just pick an area of the flat that we each clean, or make a roster and clean an area each week? What do you think?" Shanice asked.

"I say a roster. It wouldn't get boring doing it like that, you know just cleaning one area. So, let's see, where's the calendar?"

Ruth got up and took the calendar off the cupboard door.

"We have 3 weeks left in this month. We have the kitchen, bath and living room. I think that we can each tidy the bedroom together every couple of days, right? So who wants the bath?"

They had a laugh picking duties, and then went on making their lists.

"What about friends? I say no friends after 9 at night." Ruth thought this was a good idea. Both Lizzy and Shanice seemed to think that she was some sort of alien, however.

"What, are you mad? We did not leave our parents' homes to have social restrictions girlfriend. I am not going to be telling my friends that they have to leave at 9. Tell me you're joking?" This was Shanice's opinion.

"Well... all right. Nine may be a bit early. So what time then?" Ruth still thought that nine was an appropriate time, but seeing that she was out voted, she decided that it was better to acquiesce.

"Why do we have to have a time? I mean, if we have to work, or if we have an early class the next day, then naturally we would let our friends know, and hopefully we won't have to ask them to leave. But I don't think that we should tell them that we have a time rule. They may never come back Ruthie." Shanice quickly got this point across.

Ruth didn't really like the sound of this, but she decided that once the noise was not so loud that she couldn't sleep, then people could leave whenever they wanted. She relaxed a bit once that thought sank in. She even felt that she was being a bit uptight over the whole matter. She must remind herself that she was not her parents.

"So, that's sorted. What's next ladies?" Shanice wanted to know. "I say we have a party to celebrate our freedom. As a matter of fact, I already made out a list of people to invite."

"A party? That's a bit extreme? I was thinking that we should celebrate by going out to have a curry. The restaurant on the corner is not expensive; they have three-course meal deals, and the woman in the Laundromat said that the food tastes great." Ruth thought that she was convincing. She didn't like the idea of having a party at the flat.

"A curry? Oh Ruth, you are beginning to sound like my Nan. We can always have a curry, but a party will launch us as the independent set. Do you know we are the only ones from Yr 11 and college who live alone? Think of how popular we'll be if we have a party and our friends see that we live alone. They'll think that we are sorted: a flat, jobs and uni? How much better does it get than that? So, are we going to vote on a party? What do you think Lizzy?"

"Well, I think that both your ideas are pretty good. A curry is good to start with. We don't really have a lot of money to spend on a party, and we don't want the neighbours to think that we will be noisy and troublesome. Maybe we can leave the party till after the first semester, or even the first year of uni when the weather is nicer, and we can have a barbeque in the back garden and invite friends we get to know better during the year. We can start with a curry and invite a few mates to come to the flat afterwards: we can have them over for something to drink."

Ruth was quick to add: "That's a brilliant idea, Lizzy! We all get what we want, save our money and have something to look forward to at the end of the first year of uni."

Shanice grumbled: "I feel that the two of you are ganging up on me, but I actually like the idea of inviting a few friends to have a curry with us then bringing them back to see the flat. It won't be a party, but they will still see that we are independent girls. So let's do it then. What do you say about next Saturday evening? We can even take pictures and put them on Facebook."

Shanice and Elizabeth agreed, and they made a list of a few friends that they would invite to have a curry with them. They also made a shopping list of snacks and refreshments that they needed for after the curry. They were quite excited.

"So what else?" Shanice said. "What else are we going to put on our list of do's and don'ts? What about boys?"

"What do you mean by boys?"

"Well, you know, can boys come over?"

"I don't see why not. But who are these boys anyway? Not just a boy you meet at the tube station, I hope. I know how crazy you can be Shanice."

"Sure. I'm the crazy one. I mean. Can we have our boyfriends over?"

"Seeing that I don't have one, that won't be a problem with me. The answer is no. And the last time we spoke Lizzy didn't have one either. Who is your flavour of the month Shanice? Are you still mad for Josh?"

"That loser? No way! He was getting a bit boring. All he wanted to talk about were the apps on his phone, and his games console. He was cute, but boring." She pulled a funny face, and the girls laughed.

"So who are these boys you want to have over?"

"Nobody in particular; but I just want to know if we have a friend who is a boy, can we bring him back to the flat?"

"I say no." Ruth added quickly. "I don't mean to generalise, but sometimes boys and girls communicate on different levels. A girl may just want a friendly ear to chat to, like another girl, but a boy may think that she is interested in a relationship. If you bring a boy back here who you think is a casual friend, he may think that it is an invitation to be intimate. I say no."

"I say no to strangers Shanice. If you only just met a boy and end up chatting with him, and he makes you laugh, that does not mean that you can invite him over. Let's only have people over we know really well: boys and girls. Like Brandon from college. He was really nice, and a lot of girls said that he was polite and friendly."

"Yeah. You know why, don't you? He was gay."

"No Shanice. He was just a nice person. Just because a boy is decent and polite doesn't mean he is gay. Maybe he was a Christian."

"You would know. I think that if I pay a third of the rent I can make a decision to bring a friend back to the flat. It's not as if I want to take the boy into the bedroom, or anything like that. Come on girls, lighten up."

"But Shanice, how can you want to bring a boy you hardly know back to our flat? Suppose he has other motives in mind, and he gets carried away. What will you do then?"

"What! You mean apart from saying no and giving him a good,

hard push, and screaming? By the time I begin to scream I am sure he'll be halfway down the stairs. Don't worry; you know I can take care of myself. I'm bringing boys back to the flat. It'll be all right. Trust me."

Ruth began to have a sick feeling in the pit of her stomach. Was Shanice going to be a problem? All of a sudden she realised what her Aunt Ellen meant when she used to say that you never really knew a person until you lived with them. At school Shanice was always the life of any group she was in, and people gravitated towards her because of her outgoing personality. She was bubbly and fun, and what Ruth liked about her was that she didn't really judge people. She had this thing she used to say that everyone deserved a chance because you never knew what they had been through in life. Ruth embraced this, because it reminded her of the ministry of Jesus Christ. But, now she was seeing a totally different side of Shanice that appeared to be spoilt, manipulative and wanting to have her own way. She would have to remember to pray about this. She felt uneasy about bringing boys back to the flat, but if Shanice made her mind up, she and Lizzy would have to work around that. What would her cousin Lisa do? She would call and ask her later.

"Here's one for you old grannies." Shanice added. "I say no alcohol."

"Why not? I don't see anything wrong with a few alcopops. I've had those before, and they are nice, especially the strawberry ones. I think that hard liquor should be banned, but a few alcopops never hurt anyone." Lizzy said.

This time Shanice and Ruth looked at each other. It seemed like they really didn't know each other very well after all. Who would have thought that Lizzy drank? Sweet, kind Lizzy, who could also be a little shy.

"Well, if Miss Shanice can have boys over, then a few alcopops shouldn't be a problem. What else girls? Should we check out the local drug dealer and get some spliffs?" said Ruth.

Both Shanice and Lizzy shouted "No!"

"But you know what I would like?" added Ruth, "I would like a prayer and discussion session with you girls. I think it would be nice if we could sit together and pray, and then talk about parts of the Bible."

Shanice was quick to say "It's been a long time since I've been to church, and all I know about the Bible is what I remember from Sunday school and RE classes and I was asleep for most of those. What am I expected to share?"

"Well, we could read a passage before getting together, a short one Shanice, don't worry, and we could talk about what we think. I mean, I don't know loads. Just because I go to church doesn't mean that I don't still have a lot to learn."

"I can tell you now, that you know a whole lot more than me. But, you know what? It's only fair that since I can have boys over, and Lizzy can have her alcohol, then you can have your religion." And she laughed sarcastically.

"Lizzy? Are you ok with this?" Ruth asked.

"Yes. I think it's cool to be honest. I didn't go to church because my mum never went, but I am curious to know something about God apart from what I got from my sceptical mother. Yeah, then let's do it. When is the first session, and what do we have to read. By the way, you know we don't have Bibles, don't you?"

"Don't worry, as you know, you can find anything on the Internet. You can use your laptops or even phones to look up the passage. Let's start with Genesis 1, verse 27, Genesis 2, verses 16 and 17, and Genesis 3, verses 1 to 6. I'll write them down for you. I think you'll enjoy that; especially you Neecie."

Shanice rolled her eyes as if to say 'oh bother!' then she smiled.

After their meeting they decided to take a walk. It was a really nice evening, and they did not want to spend the whole day in the flat. They put on their jumpers and went out.

So after the initial agreement on cleaning, and other affairs to do with their living arrangements, they spent the rest of the day discovering their new neighbourhood. All's well that ends well. Ruth found herself wondering what her family was doing. She wished they could be with them exploring the neighbourhood. She would have to remember to call them later.

CHAPTER 3

DO I REALLY KNOW MY FRIENDS?

[7] Love bears up under anything and everything that comes, is ever ready to believe the best of every person, its hopes are fadeless under all circumstances, and it endures everything [without weakening]. 1 Corinthians 4:7 (Amp)

Ruth had to admit to herself that even though she was still quite excited to be living away from home, she was finding it somewhat challenging. She would have never guessed that this was what couples, especially if they had children, had to do to make ends meet. Juggling a job and school, even on a part-time timetable was not easy at all.

She and the girls were now living together for a month. Mum's delicious packed meals were long done, and she sometimes found that she could only muster the energy to prepare a sandwich at the end of the day. She also noticed the same with Lizzy and Shanice. Once a week, one of them would try to make a simple, hot meal so that they could sit together and enjoy it over a nice, long chat about what was going on at school.

They saw each other at uni mostly only when they were passing each other in the hall. They did manage to take one class together, so it was good to sit together, and be able to share notes. Apart from this brief time together at school, they either had to rush off to work, or other classes.

She understood better why her parents were so concerned about her grades suffering. Age really does bring wisdom, and of course experience. She made up her mind that if either Hannah or Jonathan wanted to follow in her independent footsteps, she would talk them out of it. She even wondered whether she would decide to move back home after the first year of living together. These thoughts came at the end of long, hard days. On days when her schedule was not as hectic, she could see the light at the end of the tunnel, and had no thoughts of going back home, although she wondered about how much more difficult it would be when she took up her full-time timetable. She made up her mind that she would work really hard to get a full scholarship, so she would only have to work to pay her part of the rent and household bills. Each time she considered her new life, she appreciated her parents all the more.

As she put her key in the lock, she heard laughter coming from inside the flat; not just laughter, but also a man's voice. She stopped, listened, and pushed opened the door tentatively. When she entered the living room she stopped, and her jaw dropped. She saw Mr Caledonia, their Graphic Arts professor from uni sitting on the sofa with Lizzy. There were notes spread out on the centre table in front of them, and a few bottles of Lizzy's famous alcopops. She was flabbergasted and could not even muster up her regular pleasantries when greeting people. She just nodded and went into the bedroom. She sat on her bed and decided to call Lizzy and ask what a professor, a male professor was doing sitting in their flat. Shanice wanted to invite boys home, but Lizzy beat her to it by bringing home a man. Was she over-reacting? It was obvious that they were doing work, evidenced by the notes scattered about. And, they weren't even sitting close to each other suggesting that there was anything else going on, but there were the alcopops.

Ruth had done her research on alcopops and found out that there was 4.5 to 6% of alcohol in each bottle. There was between 2 to 12% in beer, depending on the brand, and 9 to 16% in wine. So she realised that like anything else, the quantity consumed could greatly affect the perception of the person drinking them. She didn't know if Lizzy had anything to eat. She did seem to be laughing louder than usual, which could mean different things, two of which were that she was drunk, or that she fancied Mr Caledonia. From what Ruth remembered, his jokes in lectures weren't that funny. She was beginning to be somewhat concerned. He must have been at least 38 years old, maybe even 40! And she got the impression that he was married.

She took a deep breath, and was about to call Lizzy when she realised that she was about to enter into a battle without praying. She quickly repented and dropped down on her knees and asked God for the wisdom to deal with the situation in the correct manner. She also asked the Holy Spirit to guide her so that she would know exactly what to say.

"Lizzy." She called.

"Ruth. Are you calling me?"

"Yes. Sorry. Can you come in here for a minute?"

She heard Lizzy excuse herself, and walk to the bedroom. She would have to remember to lower her voice just in case Mr Caledonia heard their conversation. Lizzy entered the room, and she could tell by her eyes that she was drunk. Ruth hoped that she would make sense to her.

"Lizzy, what's he doing here?" she asked.

"What Brian? He's just helping me with some work I didn't understand. Cool huh?"

"No Lizzy. Not cool. He is our professor. Does that not seem a bit odd to you? And since when are you calling him Brian?"

"He told us we could call him Brian on the first day of class, remember?"

"Maybe I didn't think it was appropriate to be calling my professor by his first name. Look Lizzy, I can tell that maybe you had too much to drink. Did you eat anything?"

"Look Ruth, you are not my mother for heaven's sake! Stop acting as if you are! I'm fine. I'm going back outside. Brian has a lecture tonight so he can't stay for much longer. Actually you are cutting into my study time, mum." And with that she left the room.

Ruth wasn't so sure if that went very well. At least he wasn't going to be staying for much longer. She was hungry, but was in no mood to go into the kitchen with them there. What was she thinking? This was her home too, and maybe she could get Lizzy to eat something. She went outside and into the kitchen. Opening the fridge she saw that there was ham, cheese and lettuce. She would make a batch of sandwiches and just go out into the living room and offer them some. She would also sit there with them eating hers. It sounded like a good idea in her head. She would have to try it out and see if it worked. Lizzy was her friend, and she would treat her like one. No way was she going to abandon her at the first sign of trouble or conflict. What sort of friend would she be if she did that?

She made up a batch of ham and cheese sandwiches, and took a few cans of cola out of the fridge and put them on a tray with some fruit and took them outside.

"Whatever you're doing looks like hungry work. I made us some sandwiches. Hello Professor Caledonia. Excuse my manners, I don't think I said hello when I came in. Have a sandwich and some cola. Let me go get some serviettes." And she went back into the kitchen, more to breathe than to get serviettes. When she went back into the living room, she was relieved to see that they were both eating, and drinking. Lizzy was on her second sandwich by the looks of it. Ruth thanked God for showing her what to do.

They ended up chatting and the atmosphere lightened a bit. Ruth was still not so sure about having a man, their teacher in the flat, especially since it was clear that Lizzy had some sort of crush on him. All she could do was try to talk some sense into her, and see what happened at their next meeting which just happened to be the next day. Actually if Shanice got home early that evening, she would call one to discuss the Professor Caledonia matter. She was curious to see what Shanice would say.

Professor Caledonia finished his sandwich and cola, and left. Lizzy looked at Ruth, then walked up to her and gave her a hug.

"Thanks Ruthie." She said. "I'm really sorry. You are a good friend."

"No worries. I know you would do the same thing for me if the tables were turned."

"What are you talking about? We can't even get you to think of dating, but you are going to bring a male teacher back to the flat? What did you put in those sandwiches?"

Ruth cleared the food off the table while Lizzy lay on the sofa.

"What have I done Ruth?"

Ruth dropped the tray and looked at her. "What do you mean 'what have I done?' What *did* you do Lizzy? Did that man do anything to you?"

"No. No. I just mean telling him that we could work here. We were at school in the Graphic Arts room, and he was showing me some work, and all of a sudden I asked him if he wanted to work at home."

"But he didn't have to say yes, did he? Look Lizzy, I think we should talk about this when Shanice comes home. We did say that we would discuss everything together and not leave anybody out. This is a whole other level of list-making here that we never expected. I'll call her and ask what time she'll be home."

When Shanice returned home at around 20:00, she could hardly wait to have a meeting. Ruth told her briefly what she wanted to discuss, and she was beside herself with curiosity over what Lizzy had done.

She sat on the sofa and said: "So, what exactly happened here today? Did you say that California was in our flat with Lizzy?"

"Calm down Shanice. This is serious. Lizzy you should explain."

"Well, it was after class and Brian, Professor Caledonia, was helping me with some work I didn't understand. I really like him. He is funny and kind and I look up to him. I think that he is very special for wanting to give me extra help."

Ruth and Shanice looked at each other. "You know that in a way that's his job, and the only reason that he doesn't do it for other people is because they don't ask. He isn't doing anything out of the ordinary Lizzy. Surely you know that?"

"Well, ok, but he is so sweet. He makes me feel as if he really cares if I do well."

"Stop right there. The man is a teacher. Ok. Sorry a professor, but still a teacher at the end of the day. If he didn't want you to do well, that would be a problem. He is only doing what his job description says." Shanice quickly added.

"Look. I think that he is nicer to me than he is to other students."

"Then this is a problem. He isn't supposed to show favouritism. He could get into trouble for that."

"Not really Shanice. At least I don't think so. If one student is keener to do well than another, and he helps them more, then that is ok. But I think that he realises that Lizzy may have a crush on him, and is taking a bit of advantage. What was he hoping to achieve by coming back to her flat? Do you think that if she lived with her parents he would do that?" Ruth said.

"Not really." Lizzy said. "But I do like him...a lot."

"Isn't he a bit old for you?" Shanice asked.

"And a bit married?" Ruth added.

"He isn't really married. Well, that's what he said." Lizzy corrected them.

"How does a person end up not *really* married? The last time I checked, it's either they are, or they aren't. So explain this to me Liz." Ruth was beginning to worry.

"Ok. I did ask him about if he was married, and he said that he and his wife are on a break because they weren't getting along. They still talk and she has their daughter."

"Elizabeth Richards you cannot really be so naive. I thought I was the inexperienced one here." Ruth said. "Listen. He is married. He has a wife, and they are not divorced. That means that he is married. And how do you know that he is telling you the truth anyway? Suppose his wife is living abroad, or even on a holiday. Just because you have a schoolgirl crush on this man, doesn't mean that your brain has stopped working. Think Lizzy."

"I think Lizzy is looking for a father-figure in her life. You know she has issues going back to when her dad left her and her mum, and ever since then she is still looking for dad."

"Psychology 101, eh Shanice? Can't you two just understand that I like the man? What's wrong with that? It's not harmful, and we aren't hurting anybody. Ok, so, I'll ask him again about his wife, but what's wrong with liking someone older?"

"First of all the two of you don't have too much in common. If you do decide to get to know someone you should be able to relate to them on many levels. You have to agree that apart from the fact that you laugh at all his corny jokes, and you both like Graphic Arts, you probably have very little, or nothing else in common."

"Yeah. What kind of music does he like? And does he know anything about video games, and young people stuff. He is too old for you, and to be honest I think he is taking advantage of the fact that you drink, Lizzy. Did you consider that? Suppose he asks you to work at his house the next time? Would you go? And suppose you did decide to go, and started to drink...then what? You do know that alcohol stops your ability to think straight don't you?"

"You know what? This reminds me of the night I sat with my parents over dinner telling them that we had made plans to move in together. I already had my mind made up, and all they could say was that they didn't like the idea, but that they couldn't do anything short of tying me in the house." Ruth said. "Lizzy. It sounds like you fancy this man. All I can say is that it is not right. It is not a healthy relationship. I think like Shanice says he is just taking advantage because he knows you like him, and he knows now that you lose control when you drink. I will say here that I hope you aren't planning on sleeping with him. That is called fornication, and it is wrong."

"I don't even know what I am planning on doing. And, why is it wrong anyway. Isn't it a way for two people to show that they care for each other? What's the big deal anyway? If two people love each other, then what's the problem?"

"First of all, we're getting off the subject a bit. Let's keep the discussion orderly, and not jump all over the place. We called this meeting to talk about your relationship with Professor Caledonia. Let's finish that first then maybe we'll talk about why fornication is wrong afterwards. Ok?" Ruth said.

"Yes. I agree, because I also want to know what's wrong with expressing physical love for someone you care about." Shanice added.

"Well. I care about Brian."

"Wait a minute. Wait a minute. How long have you known him? What...two, three weeks during lectures, and maybe a few individual after school sessions? How can you care for him already? You don't even know him." Shanice was making a fair bit of sense tonight. It seems as if she knew somewhat more about relationships than Lizzy. This at least, was a relief. Who knew that it would be Lizzy they would have to be looking out for.

"You know that sometimes you just know something, and you can't explain it? It is usually like this with feelings."

"Well I'll tell you what I know about feelings and relationships. My experience with them in my very dysfunctional family is based upon what wasn't there, and what my mother complained about after the fact. She used to say 'things would have been a lot better in this family if your father didn't leave me to raise you children on my own.' So from that I learned that families probably run smoother with two parents. Oh, and another thing she used to say was 'no money, no love' and I think she meant sex. When she said that I used to think that without money people didn't feel good enough about themselves or each other to want to be all cuddly, and lovey-dovey. Ruthie could probably tell you a lot more because of what she saw her parents do. Right Ruthie?"

"Well, I know what you mean. My parents, as you two know were raised Christian, and had to go to counselling for a long time before they got married. By then they knew that they were meant for each other, and that they wanted to start a family together. There was never any thought of them living together before getting married. To cut a long story short, the Bible is their manual for living, and raising a family. Don't get me wrong, this doesn't mean that there weren't difficult times and arguments, but they were solved according to biblical principles. I loved growing up in my family. The strictness that I used to complain about in secondary school wasn't because they were hard and unfeeling, I complained because they would never deviate from what the Bible said on all issues. Apart from that, they are really loving parents, who care one hundred percent about my welfare."

"Lizzy, I can't argue with what you think you are feeling, but just because you get a warm, tingly sensation when you are around Professor Caledonia doesn't mean that you are ready for a meaningful relationship with him. It is probably just that you are lusting after the man. Lust is not love, it only satisfies the flesh, scratches an itch to put it in baser terms. Just be careful. Friendship is healthy, but find out more about him before you start losing your head, ok?" Ruth got up and gave her a hug.

Lizzy pouted but shook her head in agreement.

CHAPTER 4

PROBING QUESTIONS AND AGE OLD ISSUES

Then you will know the truth, and the truth will set you free." John 8:32 (NIV)

The next evening they were going to have their first Bible discussion. They had planned on having one every week, but their schedules prevented them from being able to do so until now. Ruth prayed that she would be able to answer any questions that her friends may have had; but she would be truthful and let them know that she didn't know the answer if that were the case.

They began by taking turns to read the Scriptures that were chosen: they were all chosen from Genesis. After the reading Ruth asked if they had any questions.

"Of course we have questions Ruthie. We want to challenge you about God. Actually we want to know what makes you so different."

"Yeah, but you didn't say 'different' did you, Shanice. You said 'weird'".

They all laughed out loud. "Never mind, I still love her. So what do you want to know?"

"What does it mean that we were made in God's image? Does He have two eyes, hands, a neck, toes and the whole lot?"

"The Scripture says in John 24 that God is a spirit. So if God is a spirit and we were made in His image, then we are spirits living in a suit made of earth. If you look at Genesis 2 verse 7 it shows how God made man out of the dust of the ground. But the Bible does also speak of the eyes of God, His heart, and the fact that He hears, implying that there are ears."

"I went to my Nan's funeral two years ago, and they said 'dust to dust, ashes to ashes,' was this what the priest meant? That nan was made from dust so that she was going back to dust?" asked Lizzy?

"Yep. That's right. Our bodies go back to the earth."

Shanice spoke up and asked: "So what happens to our spirit, then? Since it comes from God, does it go back to Him? I think that's the answer, Ruthie."

"Well...it's not as simple as that, but I'll give you the short answer, and maybe another day we can get into the fuller explanation."

"What? You are beginning to scare me Ruth. Is this where you say that we go to hell?"

"Remember that this is the short answer. Yes. Some souls will be with God in heaven, and some will perish. We'll talk more about this in another session."

"No Ruth. Let's talk about it now. I don't want to go to hell. What do I have to do not to go to hell?" Shanice seemed scared.

"You have to be born again: give your life to Jesus." She looked at them. They both sat on the sofa, dumbfounded. They had had this conversation before, and both Lizzy and Shanice refused. It wasn't an absolute refusal, but they said that they would consider it and definitely do it at another time. When exactly, neither one was sure about. Now here it was again.

"So if I give my life to Christ next week, then I will go to heaven?"

Ruth could see that they wanted short, sharp answers to questions that could only be done justice to with longer, clearer definitions.

"Well? Will I?" this was Shanice again.

"Shanice, the answer is yes..."

"But? I can tell that there is a 'but', Ruth."

"Well. You know. The answer is yes, yes; if you give your life to Jesus, you will spend eternity in heaven." Shanice hoped that she wasn't being irresponsible by not telling them about the quality of life that they would have to live, but she quickly thought that if they accepted salvation, the Holy Spirit would do his part in transforming their minds. She didn't want her friends to think that they could just say the prayer of salvation then continue living their lives as if nothing had happened.

"So are you going to become born again now?"

"Not really." Lizzy said. I can wait a few weeks, can't I? She wanted to continue seeing Brian, and felt that if she became saved she would have to stop seeing him. She thought within herself: "Does this mean that seeing him is wrong? Because if I felt that the relationship was ok, then there would be no problem having Jesus as my Lord and saviour." Lizzy was confused, but still decided to hold her ground.

Ruth didn't want to have to say what she was going to say next, but she figured that this may be the only way to get the message through to them, at the cost of sounding really hard. "And what if you were to die today? Where would that leave you?"

Both Lizzy and Shanice shouted "Ruth!"

"What sort of a person says something like that Ruth? And you call yourself a friend." Shanice added.

"Exactly! It is exactly because I love and care about you that I said it. Look. I know I weirded you out, and it was not the sort of thing a friend usually says to another, but I just want to point out to you that putting off salvation is playing Russian roulette with your life. Turn to Romans 10 verses 9 to 10 in your Bibles."

Shanice used her phone to find the Scripture, and Lizzy thumbed through the Bible not knowing where to look. Ruth moved closer to her on the sofa, and showed her where to find the verses. "Thanks Ruth." Lizzy said, coyly.

"No worries. Could you read it for us?"

Lizzy read: "that if you confess with your mouth the Lord Jesus and believe in your heart that God has raised Him from the dead, you will be saved. For with the heart one believes unto righteousness, and with the mouth confession is made unto salvation."

"Here, I'll read you a couple more Scriptures to back this up, because the Bible says in 2 Corinthians 13 verse1, that 'In the Mouths of 2 or 3 Witnesses Shall a Thing Be Established'. That just means that when God wants you to pay attention to something important that He has said, it can be found in a few places in the Bible."

While Ruth was finding the Scriptures, Lizzy whispered to Shanice: "This is serious, isn't it Neecie? Are you going to do it? You know...the salvation thing."

Shanice whispered back: "I am considering it. I don't want to end up in hell. I get the feeling it isn't a good place to be. What about you?"

"I am afraid. I don't want to stop seeing Brian, and I feel that if I am saved, I may have to."

Ruth found two more verses: "Right, in Acts 16:31 it says 'and they said, "Believe in the Lord Jesus, and you will be saved, you and your household." then in Mark 16:16 it says 'Whoever believes and is baptized will be saved, but whoever does not believe will be condemned.'" She looked up at them, and wondered if she had done the right thing. They both looked a bit worried.

"Lizzy? Shanice? Are you ok?"

"I don't want to die, Ruth."

"I did not say you were going to die. But we are all going to die some day, anyway. You do know that, don't you?"

"I mean I don't want to die now." Lizzy said.

"That's not what Ruth is saying, Lizzy. Get Brian out of your head, and pay attention, will you. It looks as if the bottom line is either we accept Jesus and be saved, or we don't and perish after death. Our bodies go back to the earth, and our souls go either to heaven or hell depending on the choice we make. Right Ruth?"

"In a nutshell, yes. Look. Answer these questions: do you believe in God?"

Shanice replied: "I think so, but I have never seen him or anything, like you."

"I have never seen Him, either, but I know that He is real."

"How come you never saw him, and you believe in him? That makes no scientific sense."

"Yeah. That's right." Lizzy piped in, feeling a bit more confident that she seemed to be able to use an infallible scientific proof in the argument.

"Well. Have you ever seen oxygen?"

"No, but that's different." Lizzy argued.

"No, actually it's the same argument. You are saying that my belief in God should be based upon seeing Him. Well, we need oxygen to survive and we have never seen it, but we do however know that it is there, because without it we would be brain dead in about three minutes."

"Ok, you do have a point. But I suppose I want to know, how you know that he's there. We know that oxygen is there because we are breathing it in and we are alive. I believe God exists just because I have heard it so many times, and I suppose that in some part of me I am afraid to believe otherwise. But my belief is based upon a received notion of what other people say, but I have never had a personal experience of God. Do you understand what I am saying?"

Lizzy continued: "Take for instance Santa Claus. When I was a kid I honestly thought that he was real. Ok, maybe that's not a good example because I used to see a lot of people dressed as Santa. Why don't we say the Easter Bunny or the Tooth Fairy? I really believed in them but never saw them. But even though I never saw them, I had chocolates and money supposedly delivered by them. Then of course it was only when I was a certain age I realized that it was all made up. But at least even though I never saw them, there was something tangible that was given to me by them, in the person of my mum."

"I know what you are asking. With God it all has to do with faith. Because I believe in Him, I believe the Bible. I don't think that it is a bunch of fairy stories. So because I believe what the Bible says, I have an example of the things He has done and said. Do you believe that you will get married and have kids some day?"

Lizzy was quick to answer: "Yes I do." And she blushed.

"Well, how do you know that it is going to happen? You have no absolute assurance do you?"

Lizzy thought about this a while, and the smile left her face.

"I see where you are going with this Ruth." Shanice said. "You are saying that because we see the examples of other couples out there who get together, marry and have kids, we have the belief, or faith that the same thing can happen to us, and if we really hold on to those thoughts they can happen."

"Exactly! That is faith!"

"Wow! I never thought I would be saying this, but I am enjoying this. You make it so real Ruth. Do you guys remember Miss Heathergrove in Year 9 RE? Oh man, she was a drag. I blame her for losing all interest in anything to do with religion."

They laughed. "Maybe so, but ultimately it was your decision not to pursue it." Ruth said. "But you haven't said whether you believe in God Shanice."

"You know Ruth; I'm with Lizzy on this one. I kind of believe that there is some huge, great power out there holding everything together, and when I look at nature and animals and so many things I think that this huge power must be what people call God. I think that some of the theories about the way the universe was formed make no sense at all, even for a cynic like me. I mean how can I believe that everything just came together in some big explosion? My problem with this is that it should still be happening. See what I mean? Why did it only happen one time? But that's me. I'm no astrophysicist."

Shanice went on: "When I was little my mum used to make me go to church with my Nan. Kids like anything so it wasn't too bad, but once I was a teenager I refused to go. I must admit though, that the only reason I stopped was because some of my friends used to laugh at me, and tell me that I was a goody two shoes, and I wanted to be their friend more than anything. So the pressure won out over church. Then too some church folk are so boring. It's hard to think that they know how to have fun."

"That's too bad, but all that takes us back to the topic of salvation. Do you think that you are ready to accept Christ as your savior today?"

"I am sorry, but I will wait a while. I'll use faith, and believe that I won't die right now, so when I'm good and ready, I'll do it." Lizzy was still thinking of Brian. She would hate to think that if she got saved she might lose him. God could wait.

"I do want to be saved Ruth, but I'll postpone it until a little while longer."

Ruth looked at them and smiled sadly. She thought "Lord, it is not me that they are rejecting, but you. Forgive them."

After their first session, they went out for a walk and some ice cream. It was the end of another day.

Ruth decided to call Aunt Ellen and invite her to one of their sessions. Maybe the girls needed to hear her personal testimony to help them make up their minds.

CHAPTER 5

LIZZY'S FIRST DATE WITH BRIAN

---

[4] Even though I walk through the valley of the shadow of death, I fear no evil, for You are with me; Your rod and Your staff, they comfort me. Psalm 23:4 (ASV)

*L*izzy was excited. She was so thrilled that she felt a surge of electricity running through her entire body. All night she tossed and turned on her bed, hardly getting any sleep. She looked at the illuminated clock face on her mobile phone and saw that it was only 5:20 a.m. She wanted to scream. Could she last through the day?

She was finally going out on an extended date with Brian. 'Extended', because they had spent a lot of time together in the classroom, and in the cafe across from the flat. She decided that she wouldn't ask him back to the flat seeing that the girls were a bit 'freaked out' by the fact that their teacher, a man, was in the flat. They spoke at length about it, and she was out-voted: even Shanice voted against her. She thought that at least Shanice would be on her side.

She and Brian were close friends now, and she felt that after all the pep talks from her flatmates, she was sure that she could handle herself. They had discussed a lot of things that made her sit back and think seriously about whether she had made the right decision. Lizzy admitted that she wasn't the most experienced person in the world, and so, people always told her that she was naive, green and vulnerable to people who tended to take advantage of others. She had never had a boyfriend, well, she had friends who were boys, and had been to parties, but she was not as sheltered as Ruth was, and never had a boyfriend because she was just a bit shy. She was a pretty girl, but somewhat withdrawn, so she tended to fade into the background in crowds.

Nevertheless, as she contemplated the evening that she was going to spend with Brian she just had a feeling that everything would be all right. One thing she did learn to do from the prayer circles was say some semblance of a prayer every now and again. She still hadn't given her life to the Lord, though. In some ways she figured that she wouldn't be able to date Brian if she had, and a part of her really wanted to be with him. The only way she could describe her feelings toward him was that he made her feel special, and she liked that. Ruth had said that there was probably a void left in her life due to her not growing up with her father, and not even knowing who he truly was as a person seeing that she didn't have a personal relationship with him as a child, and that she needed to be completely healed from that brokenness before pursuing a relationship with a man, or any friendship as a matter of fact. She seemed to think that she, Lizzy, was looking for someone to complete or validate her, and that she should enter a relationship whole. It made sense at the time, but she did not have the energy to think about any of that now. Ruthie told her that she should always pray for wisdom in all situations, and she did a couple of times: did it work? That she was not sure of.

Brian was taking her to a Japanese restaurant. He said that he wanted to introduce her to sushi, and sake. She looked up sake on Wikipedia and found that it was a wine made from rice and that it could be served warm. She had never had sushi before, but the thought of eating raw fish did not bother her; she wanted to show Brian that she could be mature, sophisticated, and open to new experiences. She would make sure not to drink too much sake, though; she read that it was 18 – 20% alcohol. She was doing this for Ruth who was really worried about her being tipsy when Brian was at the flat. She realised that if she became too drunk this might turn him off her, and she did not want to do anything to harm their relationship. She would be crushed if he decided to dump her and start going out with another girl. If that happened she didn't think that she could remain at uni, she would definitely drop his class, and try to avoid him.

But what was she thinking? It was now 8:00 and the other girls were just getting up. Shanice had to meet friends for a study group, and Ruth was meeting her mum for lunch, so she would have the flat more or less to herself for a pampering session before leaving. Brian was stopping by the flat to pick her up in his sports car at 7:00. She bought a fuchsia Japanese kimono from a charity shop, and borrowed a pair of black bootleg trousers from Shanice for the occasion; she also picked up an ornamental hair accessory. Lizzy knew that Brian would like what she was planning on wearing and this made her smile contentedly.

The day seemed to drag by. The girls seemed a bit distant with Lizzy, but in retrospect she knew that this was a figment of her imagination. Maybe she was the one who withdrew a bit, knowing that they did not approve of her relationship with Brian, and would have preferred it if she cancelled the date. She must admit that Ruth and Shanice loved her, and did not want to see her hurt, but she reassured them that she wasn't planning on being hurt. She wished that they could take the time to get to know Brian better, but she also knew that that was a futile notion. She was exasperated about this, but knew that it was difficult for them because he taught them all. She was not sure where their relationship was going. When she allowed her imagination to get the better of her, she daydreamed that they would get married, have two children and live in a country cottage with a Jack Russell, and maybe a cat.

She used some of the products that her friends had given her for her birthday: face mask, hair food, skin softeners, for her pampering session. She would also give herself a mani-pedi. She had a bottle of nail polish called Tantalising Tomato that she hadn't yet used, and would take pleasure in applying it to her nails. A little after lunch time she prepared a light tuna salad; she was hungry, but did not want to spoil her appetite for later on. She was also able to take a nap during the mid-afternoon. This took the edge off the stress. She felt a bit jittery, but knew that when they were going on subsequent dates, this would not be the case.

Before she realised it the time passed by and it was time to prepare for the date. She took great pains to put just enough gel in her hair to keep it in place. She had found a video on the Internet demonstrating how to comb one's hair in a French roll, or 'banane' as the French called it, and followed it to the letter. Then she stuck the hair accessories – ornamental chopsticks in, to form a perfect 'V' at the top of her head.

For her makeup she decided to be subtle and understated: she wasn't crazy about heavy makeup, or tarantula-like false eyelashes. She often wondered what the attraction of putting them on so heavily was. It just looked messy and uncomfortable to Lizzy, but a lot of her friends in college and uni wore them like that, and like her mum used to say: "to each his own."

She looked at herself in the mirror and approved. By the time she was ready to leave Ruth had come back from the outing with her mum. The lunch turned into a half day of shopping and she returned with lots of groceries, and goodies. Ruth's parents were very good to them, and occasionally treated them to unexpected treats that the girls would not have thought of spending their hard-earned money on.

Ruthie looked at her, and said "Wow! You look lovely. I wish you were going out with Shanice and me. But I don't suppose I can do anything about that." Lizzy rolled her eyes.

"So then, what do the two of you have planned for after dinner?"

"You know, Ruthie. I really don't know. But I know where you are going, and I want to stop you before you go too far. I know you care, and don't want me to be hurt, but you have to trust me on this. And besides, it's not to say you can make me stay home, anyway."

"I know. But what kind of friend would I be if I didn't try until the very last minute? Please promise me that if he tries any hanky panky you won't let him. And don't drink at all, but if you can't help yourself, then just have one glass. Please Lizzy."

"I'll try my best. I think I hear Brian. See you. Tell Shanice bye when she gets back. Love you." And with that she grabbed her coat and was out the door.

Ruth immediately dropped to her knees and prayed: "Dear God, protect Lizzy. Give your angels charge over her. Give her wisdom, God.

Please don't let anything happen to her. In Jesus' name. Amen." She knew that this was not her best prayer, but she was so worried that this was all she could muster. She sat on the sofa and stared at the wall. What to do? She decided to read her Bible.

The Japanese restaurant was called Zen Garden, and it was beautiful. Lizzy had never been to Japan, but she felt as if she were there. The tables were very low, and they had to sit on mats on the floor; they also had to take their shoes off before they entered their enclosed cubicle.

Brian explained what the various selections of sushi were, and told her which ones were his favourites to help her make a choice. She ended up choosing tuna, salmon and 2 vegetable combinations: this seemed safe for a first try. Brian warned her that the horseradish paste was very spicy and had the effect of clearing the sinuses with each bite. Lizzy was particularly glad that she had not put on mascara. She could just imagine the black streaks flowing down her cheeks.

After ordering the sushi, Brian ordered a small carafe of sake for them. Lizzy was quite excited about trying this, and took a small sip. Yuk! She hated it, but smiled and said that it was interesting. She had to appear sophisticated at all costs, and maybe the taste would grow on her. Better yet, possibly the taste of the horseradish paste would overpower the flavour of the sake.

Dinner went well. She was pleasantly surprised by the sushi. It was quite tasty, although the tuna was a little fishy.

Brian told her that she looked beautiful, and stroked her hand during dinner. She liked how he paid attention to her when she spoke, and didn't dismiss anything she said. He just seemed like the perfect person for her. She felt so safe with him that she couldn't imagine him doing anything to hurt her. Once during dinner he reached over and kissed her on the cheek. She felt warm and loved. Was it love? Maybe she was thinking too far in advance.

"I was thinking that maybe you'd like to drive around the city afterwards to see the Christmas lights." Brian said to her while he was paying the bill. "It's still early, and tomorrow's Saturday."

"Oh yes! Can we really, Brian? I've been meaning to go with the girls, but we just can't seem to find the time."

"Then let's do it."

While they were walking to the car park, he held her hand, then he put his arm around her shoulder. She loved the way it felt when he pulled her closer to him as they walked in step to the car. She thought she was in heaven; surely this is what all relationships should feel like. Ruth would do well to find a boyfriend, and then she would see that it wasn't a bad thing. How was a person supposed to get married if they didn't date for a while?

As they drove through the city, he kept his hand on hers, and only released it when he changed gears. The city was beautifully lit with Christmas lights of all colours, arranged in clever designs and patterns. Lizzy thought that all she needed to complete her perfect picture was snow: how wonderful it would have been if soft, fluffy flakes began to fall, muting the lights, and adding some old-fashioned romance that she used to see on telly around Christmas time. Oh well, she would have to do without that segment of her fantasy for the moment.

The evening was drawing to a close and Brian suggested that he take her back home. It was only 22:00h and she wasn't ready to go back home. Her heart began to beat so fast that she thought that she was going to have a panic attack. What could she do to stay out longer with him? Think, think fast Lizzy! Suddenly she said: "What about a coffee before going back. I know a cool French cafe near the flat."

"All right, I'd like that. I don't want to get you back home too late. I know that your roommates are probably waiting up for you, and I don't want my place to be moved any lower down in their little black books."

"You know?" asked Lizzy.

"Well, I didn't have any proof, but you just confirmed it for me by your response."

"Oh." Lizzy felt a little foolish. Why did she have to say anything?

"I realise that they probably disapprove of me because I am older, and I am your professor. Shanice flashes her eyes at me any chance she can find. She makes me smile. That only shows that they care about you, but I do too."

"Thanks Brian. I care about you too."

"What about if you came back to my house for a coffee? Would you like that?"

Lizzy wasn't sure what to say. She wasn't expecting this at all. All of a sudden she felt like a scared little girl, but exactly what she was afraid of, she wasn't sure. Ruth would tell her not to go; Shanice would probably say the same. But she was the one here in the car having to make a decision. What should she say? She didn't want Brian to think that she was a child, but she didn't know what to say. Again she felt as though she was about to have a panic attack.

"Elizabeth? Are you all right? You didn't nod off did you? So, are you willing to stop by the house for a coffee?"

"Sorry Brian." against her better judgement, she blurted out that she would go with him to his house.

"Good. We're not too far now, just another 10 minutes or so. I make a mean coffee, and I have some great biscotti I picked up in Rome last summer." and he stroked her hand.

They drove in silence for the next few minutes, until they pulled into the driveway of Brian's house. Lizzy found herself praying: "God, please give me wisdom."

Brian took the key out of his pocket and unlocked the front door. The first thing Lizzy felt was that there was a woman's touch in the place. This unsettled her further, but she quickly reasoned within herself that his wife once lived here so there was the evidence of her decorating style.

Brian took her hand and led her into the kitchen. She sat on a stool and watched him prepare the coffee maker. He worked so effortlessly. She loved looking at him. When the coffee was brewed he poured it into fine china cups, put them into a tray with the delicious-smelling biscotti, and he took her to the living room.

They sat and enjoyed the coffee. It was full-bodied, and tasted like nothing she had ever had at the local cafe, or the school canteen. How lucky she was to have all this attention showered on her by a handsome, intelligent man. She wondered what would happen next. Brian turned the stereo player on and sultry jazz tones oozed through the speakers. Wow! Things just kept getting better and better. By this time she was more relaxed, and felt guilty for her nervousness. Brian would never hurt her. What was she thinking? They chatted a bit about school, and her other classes, then Brian said that he should take her home. What? Already? Now she felt let down. At first she was nervous about coming to his home, now she did not want to leave, but she was not about to disgrace herself by trying to stay longer. She helped him clear away, and they went to the car.

The drive home took about half an hour, and they drove in silence. When Brian stopped in front of the flat, he switched off the engine and took her hand.

"I really enjoyed your company tonight. You are a special girl. Would you like to go out with me again?"

"Of course I would love to, Brian. I had the best time ever. Thanks a lot, it was a fantastic evening, and I can't wait to do it again."

"All right then, I'll arrange something for next Friday night. I'll make it a surprise for you." And with that, he kissed her on the cheek, left the car to open her door, and walked her up to the flat.

Her perfect night was over.

When she entered the flat Shanice and Ruth were watching telly in the living room.

"So...tell all. What happened?" Shanice asked.

She recounted the events of the evening in minute detail, right up to the fact that he opened the door for her and walked her up to the flat.

"Oh, and Ruth, he didn't try any hanky-panky. I told you he was a gentleman."

CHAPTER 6

AUNT ELLEN'S COLOURFUL LIFE

Train a child in the way he should go, and when he is old he will not turn from it. Proverbs 22:6 (NIV)

Time seemed to be passing by quicker than the girls wanted it to. Life seemed as normal as they could make it: Ruth had changed jobs because her first boss was a bit too friendly, and always found some excuse to call her into his office and place his hand on her thigh. It happened twice, and she decided that she wouldn't wait around for a third time. She remembered that the first time he did it she jumped up and ran out of the small, claustrophobic space that was crammed with boxes and papers. She did not want to alarm her parents so she didn't tell them, but after the second time she called her mum and told her what was happening. The next day, her father showed up at her job, and had a word with Mr. Jackson. She did not know what he told him, but that day Ruth left the job with a month's salary. She imagined that her dad had threatened to report him to the authorities; he would not have threatened him with violence, she thinks, because of his belief in the Bible. Her current job was better but more difficult. Dad helped her find it, and she was able to have Sundays off, and so had no excuse not to attend church with them on Sundays. She tried to get Lizzy and Shanice to go with her, but they always seemed to have an excuse not to.

Lizzy was still infatuated, in Ruth's opinion, with Brian. Ruth always encouraged her to talk about their dates, and what they were doing. She was really hoping that Lizzy wouldn't end up sleeping with him; she was convinced that he was married, and keeping Lizzy in the dark about what the truth behind his situation was. She wanted to spare her the pain of deep hurt, and possibly ruining her education over a man who was already spoken for. Why couldn't he just leave her alone? But she supposed that Lizzy had something to do with that too. She was so into him that she refused to believe that he could do anything to try and hurt her.

Shanice had begun hanging around with a new set of girls from her fashion class. Ruth thought that they were all right, a bit loud and flashy, but harmless enough she supposed. She did wonder where they got all the money for their clothes, though. From the looks of it they always wore the latest labels, and also seemed to change their phones quite often. They acted and spoke very maturely, and she could see why Shanice would want to spend time with them, because she liked being with people who attracted attention; Ruth often wondered how she chose Ruth as one of her best friends. One of the girls even smoked! That was another rule they all agreed upon: no smoking in the flat. When Ruth asked Shanice where they got the money for their clothes from, she said that they had good jobs, and were planning on getting her a job too. When Ruth asked what they did, Shanice wasn't sure; she said she thought it was modeling for a small fashion magazine. This was a break that Shanice was looking for, because in her spare time she drew designs in her sketch pads, and was hoping to become a designer someday. She was an art major.

They were preparing dinner because Aunt Ellen was coming by tonight. Ruth was excited about this, not only because it had been three months since she had seen Aunt Ellen, but she knew that the girls would be intrigued by her life.

Aunt Ellen was a life coach and counsellor, and travelled from city to city speaking to groups of young people about life choices that could set you back or propel you forward. She had not always been born again like her parents, but had finally turned to Jesus when she had reached rock bottom after making a series of poor decisions, all centered around men in her life. She was not a blood relation, but had met her parents when she came to their church to speak to the youth group a few years ago. Ruth was not old enough at the time to be part of one of her seminars, but had attended one when she was in Year 11. She was riveted. How could someone so balanced and confident in the Lord have made such mistakes? But that was at a former time in her life, and as a result, she devoted her life to turning lives around. She was a pastor in charge of the youth ministry at her church, Zion's Gate. Whenever there was a special programme on at her church, Ruth would attend, and sometimes help out. Aunt Ellen was poised and not only had a beautiful face, but a lovely personality. Ruth loved her, and her parents trusted her. Hers was the only house that Ruth had been allowed to spend the night at when she lived at home: such was the esteem her parents had for her.

When she arrived Ruth ran to the door, and before she could come inside she threw her arms around her. "Hello Aunt Ellen. It is so good to see you. It's been ages."

"Yes, my sweet Ruthie, it does feel like ages. I've got presents for you girls. Where are Lizzy and Shanice?"

"Hi Aunty. How are you?" Shanice and Lizzy had met Aunt Ellen at Ruth's home before, so she was not a complete stranger to them. They had never had the privilege of attending one of her seminars though, but Ruth had spoken a lot about them. They couldn't wait to ask her questions about relationships and life in general. Lizzy especially had a few questions to ask about her relationship with Brian. They knew that they could talk to her without any fear of being put down or lectured to. Based on what Ruth said, she was honest and to the point, although she did base her answers on biblical principles. But in spite of this, Lizzy felt that she could ask questions without being made to feel like a child who didn't know what she was doing.

They sat down to dinner, and Aunt Ellen began asking about uni.

"I am really loving it. I have loads of friends and am taking some pretty interesting courses. I think that it is important to choose courses that you like."

"Yeah. I think that we are all having a good time. It's a bit stressful having to work and study, but we are getting accustomed to the routines. Not only that, we know that if we don't work, we won't be able to live away from home. It is a necessary sacrifice for the lifestyle we chose."

"You girls seem to have it all figured out. What about boys?" Aunt Ellen asked.

"Well, I am glad you brought it up. Lizzy here is dating one of our professors, and doesn't have a problem with it. Shanice and I keep telling her that he will end up hurting her, but she won't listen."

"Ruth!" Lizzy snapped. "At least let me tell Aunt Ellen about it."

"What do you think about her dating a professor Aunt Ellen? Is that ok?"

"First of all let's clear the air about certain things. You do know that I am a pastor, and that all I have to say to you will be based on what the Bible said, right. I don't want you to feel let down if I don't say what you may want to hear."

"That's all right Aunt Ellen. We know. We just want to know why certain things are wrong, when so many people are doing them."

"All right. Why don't we take one thing at a time? First of all dating by world standards usually involves serial monogamy. Couples have the idea that they gain experience and knowledge about relationships by coupling with as many people as it takes to find Mr. or Miss Right, or if not, they just date to have fun and to keep themselves from being bored or lonely."

"So how are people supposed to get to know each other without dating?"

"The Bible doesn't say anything about dating. We do accept, however, that two people who express an interest in each other will want to spend some amount of time together, maybe having a meal, or taking a walk in a park, but we try to suggest that it is not in a secluded place. Going out in a group is also a good idea."

"What's wrong with being alone together?" Lizzy asked.

"Well, first of all physical attraction is a strong power. Many couples end up engaging in acts that they hadn't planned on doing when left alone."

"But, Aunt Ellen, tell me honestly, what's wrong with going all the way with someone you are dating?" Shanice asked. Lizzy was glad she did.

"First of all the Bible forbids it. Second of all intimacy and passion can cloud a person's judgment."

"What do you mean? Can you give an example?" Lizzy wanted to know.

"Yes. Let's say that the man is emotionally or physically abusive. He may have hit his girlfriend once, and she did not like it. In her mind, she knows that this is not the type of individual she wants to spend the rest of her life with, but after he hit her, he apologizes and tells her that he is sorry. He begins to kiss her, and cuddle her. Slowly she begins to relax because the acts of intimacy upstage the physical hurt. The next day he brings her roses and chocolates and they end up in bed again at the end of the night. Deep down inside there's a part of her that is screaming 'get out of this relationship', but you see love-making feels like a panacea, a cure all, to hurting people, and women like feeling affectionate and wanted. So that is why I said that it clouds a person's judgment. A woman would most likely end up with an abusive man, because she is addicted to the making up afterwards."

Aunt Ellen continued. "We encourage couples to come to counseling sessions. Doing this enables them to try to learn as much as possible about the other person's character and moral fiber before making a decision to marry them. You see girls, marriage is a contract that one is supposed to enter into for a lifetime, not only when things seem rosy. The words 'for better or worse' carry a lot of responsibility with them."

"So are you saying that it is impossible to cuddle and not go all the way?" Lizzy asked.

"Nothing is impossible, Lizzy. What I am saying is that once you get to that point it is fairly difficult to stop. Not impossible, but quite difficult. To stop at this point would mean that one of the partners leaves and goes home. No looking back. So tell me a little bit more about Brian."

"I like him a lot. He makes me feel really special."

"He's our professor Aunt Ellen. Isn't that wrong?" Ruth asked.

"Wrong may not be the right word." They looked at each other and laughed.

"What I mean is that it seems a bit odd that he does not have someone his own age to focus his attention on. Lizzy is not a child living at her parents' home, so she too has something to do with his being able to pursue a relationship with her: he didn't force her to be with him. I think what you may be having a problems with, girls, is that teachers, carers, and people in certain positions of responsibility have a duty of care. They are not supposed to be taking advantage of their charges, but you need to remember that this is university, and technically if it were a relationship based on mutual love and care with the aim of marriage, there would be really nothing wrong with it."

"I told you. Thank you Aunt Ellen." Lizzy got up and hugged her.

"Not so fast, young lady. I'm not done yet." She hugged Lizzy back and smiled. "Do you know the full facts about this man? Is he married or not."

"Well he told me that he and his wife were having a break because they weren't getting along. He said that they split up six months ago."

"Well he is still married, and you have no right being in a relationship with him. He too has no right going after anyone while still being married. Separation is not divorce. To protect yourself from hurt and possible scandal at the university, I would like to suggest that you break off the relationship with him as soon as possible. How involved are you?"

"Well, nothing has happened yet." She looked away as she spoke.

"Lizzy, Aunt Ellen is a pastor. She operates under the guidance of the Holy Spirit." Ruth said.

"What do you mean by that?"

"That she usually knows when she is being lied to."

"Well, we haven't done much. I'm sorry Aunt Ellen for lying to you. I'm really sorry, but after all you said before, I felt a little embarrassed."

"That in itself is proof that what you are doing is not right, dear. It means that your conscience is telling you that something is not what it should be."

"But I really love him. I can't live without him."

"Yes you can. The fact that you have been physically involved with him is making you feel attached, but it is better to suffer a little heartache now, than devastation later. What happens if he reconciles with his wife?"

"I don't know. I hope he doesn't" Lizzy whispered.

"Lizzy. How could you? How could you?" Ruth asked. "Wasn't it you who used to tell us how awful it was for you and your sisters when your parents divorced, and how your mother cried for almost a year afterwards when he left. How could you want that for someone else's family?" Ruth got up and went into the kitchen to put the kettle on.

There was an uncomfortable silence around the dinner table.

"Let's go into the living room while Ruthie gets the tea and dessert ready. Why don't you help her Shanice?"

Lizzy was weeping silently at the dinner table. She felt lost. What was she going to do? She had never felt so appreciated in her life. Her friends were a great comfort, but Brian made her feel completely different. She felt like somebody when she was with him. She could give up living with Ruth and Shanice, but she could not think of leaving Brian. However, Aunt Ellen basically told her that she was dating a married man. How did she get herself into this? And more importantly, how was she going to get herself out of it?

Aunt Ellen said: "Come join me on the sofa, Lizzy."

When they were on the sofa she said, "Tell me what's wrong?"

"I feel confused Aunt Ellen. On the one hand, I hear what you all are saying, and I actually understand, but you don't know how I feel. Nobody knows."

"Well, you may be wrong there, my dear. When I was in the world, that is, not saved, I had many illicit relationships. Each one felt like the right one. I fell in love very easily, and after each one, I felt crushed, lost and broken. It wasn't until I allowed Jesus into my life that I realized what true love was."

"Yes, but did you love a married man?"

"Many." She looked at Lizzy intently. Lizzy was shocked.

"You see Lizzy, I was broken going into each one of those relationships, so I was actually looking for the men to fix me. They didn't because they couldn't. In some twisted way, they were broken too. Nobody who is truly whole would commit such a selfish act and hurt his family. And two broken people do not make one whole person. In fact they make more broken people because of all the deception, hurt, lies, fear and corrupt emotions that go into cheating."

"I'll tell you just how bad it got, Lizzy." At this point Ruth and Shanice entered the living room with tea and cakes. The kitchen wasn't far away, and they had been hearing what Aunt Ellen was saying to Lizzy. They set the trays down, poured the tea, and served the cakes.

"Please go on Aunt Ellen." Shanice said.

"I was just about saying how bad things got for me before I finally cried out to God for help. I had a relationship with a very handsome, cultured, suave man who seemed to be everything I had ever wanted, and read about in novels. He dressed impeccably, spoke several languages, had lived in places that I had always wanted to visit, and knew how to treat a woman. He would visit me with the finest wines, Russian caviar, sushi that he had kept cool for me in his air conditioned car. He also took me to the most exclusive restaurants. Every wish I had to satisfy the flesh was his command. I actually think that he was the closest I have ever come to meeting Satan: he was just that good at doing all the wrong things."

"So what was the problem?" Shanice asked. "He seems like a dream come true."

"Well, apart from the fact that he was married, he introduced me to his wife."

"What?" Lizzy and Shanice said simultaneously.

"Yes. Like I said, he was excellent at doing all the wrong things. And you know what the sad thing is? I went along with it? Mind you, I knew in my heart of hearts that this was wrong. I knew that it was wrong dating married men, but that did not stop me. This is the power of the kingdom of darkness in the life of the unsaved. Anything seems justifiable. I used to tell myself that I wasn't hurting anyone, especially if his wife didn't know that we were seeing each other. But you see, the problem with that is that he was robbing his family of time. All the time that he was spending with me, he should have been giving to his wife and children: spending quality time with them. You see, it is very important for children to grow up in a nurturing, loving environment."

"What happened after you met his wife?"

"This is where things became quite bad for me living in my selfish bubble. Do you know why he wanted me to become his wife's friend?"

"Aunt Ellen, not even me and my active imagination could come up with an answer to that one." Shanice said.

"Well, it so happened that his wife was quite lonely, she didn't have any friends in the city at all. He made sure of that because as you know, friends look out for each other, and if she had any, one of them might have seen him out on the town with his lady friends, and reported back to her. So he made well sure that she was isolated, and was in total need of him for everything, especially since she was a foreigner. So when he introduced me to her we hit it off, the wife and I, and became friends. And he basically stopped seeing me and started seeing other women."

"What? No!"

"Yes. So not only did I fall for his deception, but because I was in such a web of deceit myself, I dared not say anything to his wife about his affairs. It was awful. I also had to keep track of all the lies that we had told her for me to be able to be her friend."

"Aunt Ellen, how could this happen to someone like you? It just doesn't seem like something you would get into."

"Lizzy, this is a focal point to what I am trying to get across to you all. The reality of the matter is that nobody starts off their lives making these decisions; no young person who reaches an age when they start thinking about relationships, says to themselves 'I want to be in an adulterous partnership.' This makes no sense to you does it?"

"No, Aunty, of course not; at least I hope not." Ruth said.

"So how does a man or a woman end up committing adultery?"

"Because they are unhappy with their marriage?" Shanice said.

"This is a good starting point. You see, the truth of the matter is that the problem began long before the actual act."

"I don't get it." Lizzy said.

"The foundation of a person's life generally, but not exclusively, dictates the choices that they make throughout their formation, development, and end stages in life. If a child grows up grounded in the word of God, it is highly unlikely, mind you, I am not saying impossible, but highly unlikely that as an adult, they would make certain choices."

"Like adultery?" Lizzy asked.

"Like adultery, as well as a whole lot of other things. The sum total of our actions is based on what we were taught, or not taught as children. What we saw around us on a daily basis, and so thought was 'normal' has an impact on what we end up doing if we do not receive salvation through Jesus Christ."

Aunt Ellen paused for a while to see if the girls had any questions or comments, then she went on speaking.

"I didn't grow up seeing anyone commit adultery; however, even though I did go to church, it was more out of duty. There was no Bible study at home, and the church I went to just went through the motions, because if it were anything like my home church, Zion's Gate, there was no way that I would have even considered doing some of the things that I ended up doing. If even I went astray a little I would have had the conviction of the Holy Spirit to let me know that what I was either doing, or considering doing, was wrong. On the contrary, what I saw happening in my life, was that I found justifications to continue doing the wrong thing."

"You mean like telling yourself that you weren't hurting anyone by going out with that man?" Lizzy asked.

"Yes. Exactly. What didn't help either was that I also hung around with friends who were also unsaved. At that stage in my life, I did not have one friend who talked me out of some of the things I did. I also read magazines and books that portrayed life as one big act of lure and seduction. I attended plays, movies, and watched television shows that all seemed to reflect the life that I was leading, so I felt that they were evidence that my lifestyle was more cool, chic and elegant than purely sinful." She paused.

"You see the importance of salvation is that the Blood of Jesus washes us clean, and we become new creations in Christ. When God sees us, he sees the Blood, not us, because we are still sinners, and always will be, but our lives become transformed. There is a Scripture which says 'Do not be conformed to this world, but be transformed by the renewal of your mind, that by testing you may discern what is the will of God, what is good and acceptable and perfect.' So even though my past life was a mess, Jesus cleaned me up, and made me good enough for the Father to accept me. It is a truly beautiful experience because I know that I shall have eternal life after death."

The silence in the room was heavy and thick. There was a sound coming from Lizzy's end of the sofa and when they looked at her, they saw that she was crying again.

"Lizzy. It is not the end of the world. Actually it is quite simple. You have two choices before you: either break off your relationship with Brian, or continue seeing him. I'll give you another profoundly simple Scripture: 'Today I have given you the choice between life and death, between blessings and curses. Now I call on heaven and earth to witness the choice you make. Oh, that you would choose life, so that you and your descendants might live!'"

There was another prolonged silence.

"Have you and Shanice considered accepting Jesus Christ as your Lord and savior? That is always a good place to start, and then the Holy Spirit can help you in difficult times."

"Ruthie spoke to us about it, Aunt Ellen."

"All right, at least you know that you have that choice. I am not in the business of forcing people to accept Christ. But it is good that you know that He accepts us as we are. We don't have to try and be good for Him to love us, but we do need to invite Him into our lives, though, he won't force you either."

"So what made you decide to be saved?" Shanice asked.

"There is a long answer and a short one; I'll give you the medium version." She smiled.

"After a life of doing what I wanted, I began feeling that I needed something more than the alcohol, the parties, and the relationships. At the end of each day I was left feeling empty, but kept chasing after the high of what I thought was real life. Things came to a head when my mother died. It was the lowest I had ever been in my life. She was in one country, I was in another, and because of the reckless life I had been living, I had sabotaged my visa situation, so I could not even go home for her funeral. The night when I got the news I just began drinking, and drinking. I called some friends and three of them came by, and I just continued drinking. The next morning I felt sick and disoriented because I had spent the entire night drinking whisky. A friend and colleague of mine stopped by, and decided to take me for a long drive. This helped because it was slowly clearing my head." She stopped to reflect.

"At one point I asked him to stop the car because I wanted to be sick, and it was then I had a revelation of my future."

"What was that? Was it good?" asked Lizzy.

"On the contrary, it was very scary. While I was bent over at the side of the car I saw myself being pulled down into hell. I was standing at the edge of a pit that looked like a whirlpool, and out of it came horrendous creatures who tried to pull me in. It was quite real, girls. For a while the car seemed to disappear, and it was me alone standing at the edge of this vortex of hell with these creatures pulling at me. I actually felt afterwards, that if I had blacked out and fainted away that I would have died and hell was at the door waiting for me."

"Oh my goodness! So what happened next?!

"Well, I can't remember clearly, but I know that my friend got me back home. My life began to change after that. I did not become born again immediately afterwards, but I began to live a cleaner life. I cut out a lot of the activities I used to engage in and started thinking more about God. I eventually became saved, and have not regretted it one moment. The void I had in me has been filled, and I feel whole and clean. I no longer live a life wondering if people know what I am doing, and having to lie about what I do. That takes a lot off one's mind. I have what the Bible calls a peace that passes all understanding."

"Wow! Does that mean that you don't have any problems?"

"No. Life is life and challenges do come. But I know where to find solutions and that's not in a glass of alcohol, or a cigarette. But my dear girls the time has slipped by and I must be getting off. If you have no more questions shall we pray?"

They all stood up, and Aunt Ellen prayed a prayer that made Lizzy and Shanice feel wrapped in love, and very comforted. After this she said goodbye and left. She left her calling cards for them, and told Lizzy and Shanice that they could stop by if ever they wanted to chat, and with that she was gone.

The girls cleared up the cups and plates and went to bed filled.

CHAPTER 7

A FRIEND IN NEED

[17] And I have promised to bring you up out of your misery in Egypt into the land of the Canaanites, Hittites, Amorites, Perizzites, Hivites and Jebusites—a land flowing with milk and honey.' Ex 3:17 (NIV)

Recently Ruth began hearing that Scripture in her head again, and she still had no idea why. It seemed so random. Usually when she thought of Bible verses they would be the more popular ones that even unbelievers probably heard of; but this one…why was it popping up all the time? She trusted God, and knew that in the fullness of time, it would all come to light.

After the visit by Aunt Ellen, Lizzy and Shanice began to be more aware of the importance of being saved. They wanted it, but couldn't seem to muster the courage to commit. They kept telling Ruth that they really wanted to, but felt that they would be missing out on life: there were just so many things that they wanted to do before giving their lives to the Lord. They loved Ruth dearly, but secretly found her life dull. She was a great person who could laugh at jokes -clean ones, and was generally warm, kind and caring. They felt a genuine love for her, but in reality, they wouldn't trade her life for theirs. Actually they often wondered how come she moved in with them. Each time they asked her she would say, "Never you mind that. I promise to tell you some day," and she left it there. Shanice was so glad when they were making plans to move in together that Ruth decided to make the move with them. She knew that her parents would be against it, so deep down in her heart she didn't think that she would end up being able to, but when she called saying that she had told them, Shanice was quite surprised.

So convinced were Shanice and Lizzy that Ruth was not going to be allowed to move out, that they had convinced their mothers to help them with the rent: this was the only reason they were able to take a full-time study load, and not work extra hours. When the news came that Ruth was really going to join them, Shanice began to plan on how she could get Ruth to be more like them: to loosen up a bit, and live a little, maybe go to clubs and parties with them, but to date they were unable to convince her to do either. The most she was willing to do was have a meal out, or go for a walk, and the only movies she was willing to see were the ones with no swearing, or allusions to sex. She didn't even watch certain television shows because of the topics and attitudes portrayed. So in the end, all that happened was that Ruth was no longer living at her parents' house, but nothing else about her had changed. Amazing!

Both Shanice and Lizzy had gone to see Aunt Ellen alone to discuss certain issues with her, each time leaving with the promise of giving their lives to Jesus.

Christmas was about a month away, and the girls were planning a dinner for a few of their friends. Each of them was inviting three friends so as not to have too many people in the flat at once: they figured that twelve people were a manageable number both for the food budget and the traffic through the flat. They planned to spend Christmas at home with their families. While they liked living alone and sharing space with each other, they wanted to be at home for the holidays. Ruth was anticipating this and couldn't wait to take all the presents that she had been buying for her family. She knew that mum and dad would say that she should be saving her money, but she was excited to share all she had for them, with them.

Planning the party was fun; they bought a small Christmas tree and decorated the flat with things they purchased at the local Pound Shop. They made alcohol free punch, and bought party food already set out on decorative platters. They really didn't spend that much money, but the place looked like a million pounds. How festive it looked!

Their friends started arriving at 6:00 and they brought along presents for the gift swap that they were going to do later on. The music spanned the generations, from Nat King Cole to Hip Hop Christmas; there was also a variety of world music with a Christmas twist.

They were having a great time, when all of a sudden, there was a crash in the kitchen. All the guests stopped chatting and dancing and ran into or towards the kitchen. Katy, one of Shanice's friends, was on the floor with a few hard plastic containers scattered around her. Ruth had to ask people to go back into the living room in order to give her room. She also said that nobody should try to get her to stand up until they knew what the problem was: she was glad she remembered something from her First Aid classes. Mum had insisted that this was a good thing for the whole family to learn, and so she signed them up, with the understanding that they renew their skills every couple of years.

Lizzy took a large paper plate and began fanning her, and Shanice wet a cloth with cold water and began to gently mop her forehead. After a few minutes Katy regained consciousness, and sat up slowly. At first, when she opened her eyes, she looked a bit dazed, but soon regained full consciousness, and sat up. She asked for a drink of water. When she seemed stronger Ruth and Shanice helped her into the bedroom where they had her lie down on Shanice's bed. Then, she began to talk.

"What happened to me?"

"You fainted K." Shanice told her. "How are you feeling now? Should we call an ambulance for you?" Shanice was worried. Ruth left the room to get more water.

"No, Shanice. Don't do that. You know why I fainted. Did you say anything?" Katy asked in a whisper.

"No, Katy. I wouldn't do that, but you may have to say something soon. It won't remain a secret forever you know."

"No, but by then I won't have to say anything. You know what I plan on doing. That's why you can't say anything to anybody, especially your roommate Ruth. She's so religious."

"I wish you would reconsider. That's not the only choice you have, and you know that too."

"What, so I must give up my job just because of this baby? To work I have to have a good figure, and as soon as the agency finds out they'll sack me."

"Yes. And that worries me. What kind of job fires a woman for having a baby anyway? You still haven't told me exactly what I am getting myself into. Is it just modelling you do?"

"Never you mind that. I just can't have this baby Shanice. I have to have an abortion." Just as she was saying this, Ruth walked into the room. She heard Katy's last statement.

"What? You mean you fainted because you are pregnant? That is not normal. Maybe there's something wrong with the baby, or even with you. We have to call an ambulance for you Katy." Ruth said.

"No Ruth." Katy tried not to sound too hard. "I do not need an ambulance. I'll be fine. Just leave it, ok? It'll be all right."

"And how is it going to be all right? Because you are going to have an abortion? You know I heard what you said, so don't try and cover it up. You can't be serious. What sort of decision is that?"

"It's none of your business anyway Ruth." She looked at Shanice and said, "I told you so. She and her religious ideas."

"Now you wait right there. All life is precious. All life. How can you make a decision to end a life when you don't even know whose destiny you're terminating? Your child can grow up to be a great person who makes a worthy contribution to society."

"And what if it isn't?"

"Don't think like that? Are you saying that you won't have any input into the child's life? What an individual becomes has a lot do with how they are raised. But, have you ever thought that you could give the child up for adoption, and give someone else the opportunity to love and nurture him, or her? You can't just want to flush a life down the toilet?" And then it hit her. The Scripture came back to her, and she knew at that exact moment why it had been in her head all these months. Was she receiving a prophetic word about Katy?

In the Old Testament, God gave stern warnings to the Israelites that they should not worship foreign or false gods! They were to worship Him only, the one and only true God, who created everything that was made in heaven and on the earth; He was also the one responsible for leading them out of Egyptian captivity and into the Promised Land. So why was God so adamant about not worshipping other gods, especially since He gave people a free will to do what they wanted? First of all free will is supposed to be used to do good, but not only that, some of the practices of the worshippers of false gods were an abomination to God! In the name of worship, some of them performed sexual orgies in their temples; all of the gods were made of wood, metal, stone or gold, so they were inanimate objects. Imagine what an insult it must have been to the creator of all things to worship a dead object which was unable to respond to the prayers and supplications of the people. In addition to this, one of the more profane practices involved child sacrifices: Leviticus 18:10 clearly states: "Thou shalt not give of thy seed to cause to pass through the fire for Moloch" and 18:21: "Do not give any of your children to be sacrificed to Molech, for you must not profane the name of your God…"

Molech was a bronze god that looked like a large bull. Its insides were hollow and used to start fires into which children were placed for sacrifices. Ammonites looked upon Molech as a protecting father. In Paradise Lost, Milton wrote about Molech:

"First, Moloch, horrid King, besmeared with blood
Of human sacrifice, and parents' tears;
Though, for the noise of drums and timbrels loud,
Their children's cries unheard that passed through fire
To his grim idol. Him the Ammonite
Worshiped in Rabba and her watery plain,
In Argob and in Basan, to the stream
Of utmost Arnon. Nor content with such
Audacious neighbourhood, the wisest heart

Of Solomon he led by fraud to build
His temple right against the temple of God
On that opprobrious hill, and made his grove
The pleasant valley of Hinnom, Tophet thence
And black Gehenna called, the type of Hell."
—Paradise Lost, i. 391-405

Now, as Ruth stood in the middle of the bedroom with tears in her eyes in anticipation of the fate of Katy's unborn baby, she remembered something she had learned in a Year 11 RE class when there was a debate about abortion. While researching the topic, Ruth had come across the fact that aborted fetuses are burnt, passed through the fire. She felt sick. The realization of why she had been having that verse of Scripture resonating in her head became clear. Did God want to use her to save this precious unborn child?

"Why are *you* crying?" Katy asked sarcastically. "You aren't the one who's knocked up."

"Katy. Please don't have an abortion." Ruth heard herself saying, "It's an abomination. It's wrong Katy, it's wrong. Please let me help you."

"Help me how? Isn't it a bit late for help, especially since I don't want a child."

"Is there anything that I can say to have you change your mind?"

"No…well, maybe a million pounds, and a rent –free luxury flat for the rest of my life."

"Don't joke, Katy. She's serious." Shanice said.

"And so am I Shanice. What am I going to do with a baby? My parents won't let me stay at home if they find out that I am pregnant. I know for sure my dad will say that whoever got me that way can also take care of me. So where am I going to go?"

"You know parents say all sorts of things when they are angry, but after a while they change their minds. Try them and see. Why don't you tell them?" Ruth asked.

"I don't have to. My older sister Jade got pregnant last year, and they put her out. They only saw the baby once on his first birthday, but, she is still not at home is she?" Katy explained.

"But you have a job. What if you find a place, a small place, and work until you can't anymore? Then maybe the baby's father can help support you from then on. Maybe he'll even want to marry you." Ruth said.

Katy sat still, and stared at the floor. Then she said "I don't know who the father is. Do you hear me? I don't know who the father is!" And she began to sob.

At that point Lizzy entered the bedroom. "Hey, everyone wants to know how Katy is doing." When she saw her crying she asked "Is everything all right Katy? Are you in pain? Ruth, Shanice, what's wrong?"

Shanice asked her to wait outside and to tell their guests that everything was all right. "We'll talk to you later." Lizzy left the room a bit perplexed. She hoped that Katy was ok; they all looked a bit surprised. She wondered what the matter was.

"Katy. I didn't think you had a boyfriend. How come you don't know who the father is?" Shanice asked her.

"Look. You can't say anything, ok? You can't say anything. I feel so embarrassed. But you can't tell our friends at uni. The job that I have is…well, I work with an escort agency. We are not supposed to sleep with the clients, just go out to dinner with them. The men are usually foreigners, or from another part of the country. But a couple of times the men said they would pay me more, a lot more for extra. I really don't know how I got pregnant because there was always protection."

Both Ruth and Shanice sat in silence. Neither one knew what to say. They didn't want to ask too much, but wanted to know more. Shanice was shocked because this was the 'modelling' job that Katy and the others wanted her to get into. The more she thought about it, the angrier she felt. She wondered what it was about her that made them feel that she would say yes to working for an escort agency. Was it that she liked to dress nicely, because she was friendly, that she liked to flirt a bit with boys sometimes? What kinds of unspoken signals was she sending out to people? She got up and left the room. She needed to get something to drink. She really wanted to get as far away as possible from Katy, but didn't want to overreact with the guests there. At the same time she also didn't want to seem like an unsupportive friend. If the shoe were on the other foot, God forbid, she would have wanted her friends to be supportive, not to walk away from her. In addition to that, she realized that she was only thinking about herself now, and not about how she could offer a solution that did not involve abortion to her friend. She was still angry though.

She got a glass of punch, stopped to chat with a few of their guests and to reassure them that everything was under control. She was also able to say goodbye to a few who were getting ready to leave. She looked at her watch and did not realize just how long she and Ruth had been in the bedroom with Katy. It was already twenty past midnight. A few people had already left, and only Katy's friends from the 'modelling' job were still there. From the way Katy acted, she figured that they didn't know that she was pregnant. They wanted to know if she was feeling better and whether she would be ready to leave soon. It was at this point that Shanice made a bold decision. She told them that Katy was going to stay the night, because she didn't want her having to take public transport, and paying a taxi would be too expensive. The girls asked if they could go into the bedroom to say goodbye to her, and when they had done that they left.

Spending the night would not be a problem: both sofas in the living room were folding beds so they had room for at least four more people sleeping two on a bed. They explained to Katy that they would have to let Lizzy know what was going on because it would be odd trying to whisper in such a confined living space. Katy didn't mind.

They cleared up the flat and pulled out one of the sofa beds so that Katy could lie down if she wanted to. Shanice was feeling better. Ruth was right when she said that helping people made you forget your own selfish problems. She found a pair of pyjamas for Katy. They made hot chocolate and all sat in the living room to continue their discussion.

"I think that the first thing you need to do is get yourself tested, Katy. Realistically speaking you don't know if he passed anything to you. The fact that you are pregnant clearly means that there was an exchange of fluids, so you should go to your local clinic for a test for STDs." Ruth said.

"Oh my goodness! I never even thought of that. I'll go first thing on Monday morning. How could I be so stupid?"

"Look. What's done is done. You can't go back into the past and change things now. It's too late for that. You need to find a solution to what you are going to do." Shanice said. She had found a new boldness. As she listened to herself speak, she had to admit that she was sounding more and more like Ruth.

"And an abortion should not be one of the solutions."

"But why? So many women have them all the time."

"That may be the case, but it certainly does not make it right. Abortion is taking a future life. I am not going to get into any arguments about whether the fetus is alive or not. I don't know the answer to that, but I do know that it is potentially a child. How many months pregnant are you?" Ruth said,

"About three months. Can you please tell me why abortion is wrong?"

"I know you don't want to hear me talk about the Bible, but I can't help it. The Bible says that taking a life is a sin. It is as simple as that."

"But suppose a woman was raped and gets pregnant. Is it right for her to keep that child?"

"This is what I always wondered too Ruthie." Lizzy asked. "And I know that Shanice wanted to know too."

"The way that we should live our lives is by having faith in God, and trust in Him to work things out for us. When we make up our minds on certain decisions, we are not trusting Him, but ourselves, and to be quite honest, as we can see by the state of the world, we have done a pretty poor job at that. When we decide to do as we wish God leaves us alone, because He is the one who gave us free will. He is a God of principle, so He won't just change your mind for you; He could if He wanted to, by the way. What He does is to use people and circumstances to help you try and see the truth of the situation."

"Like you telling me not to have an abortion?" Katy asked.

"You can say that. And of course, at the end of it all, you may still decide to go ahead with your decision, but you would have been opened up to different options. God can intervene in the life of your unborn child and he, or she can have a beautiful future in store. By taking the life inside you now, you are robbing its potential. I said this before."

"But it's going to be so hard." Katy said.

"But you made a decision, Katy. I am sure that things seemed easy at the time. Not only that, how do you know that it is going to be hard? You don't know that for sure. It may very well be, but then again, it may be a good experience too. You will have to rearrange your life in some major ways, but if you are truthful, you must own up to the fact that you chose this."

"No I didn't. I didn't choose to get pregnant!" Katy defended her position.

"Katy, what she means is that when a man and a woman have sex, one of the end results for the woman is pregnancy; protection or not." Shanice said.

Lizzy seemed a little uncomfortable at this prospect. She sat in silence, taking everything in. She didn't feel in a position to comment on certain things seeing that Katy was not her close friend, and like Ruth, she was not in the room when she admitted to being pregnant. She would comment when more generalized responses were needed. Not only that, she was taking everything in and thinking of her current situation with Brian.

"So if I decide to keep the baby. What will I do?" Katy asked.

"Well, I think you may have to find another job. Pregnant or not, that is not a suitable job for anybody." Shanice thought that she would make her feelings known at this point without telling her exactly how she felt about it, and her offer.

"Well, being pregnant they wouldn't keep me anyway. Where will I live?"

"I still think you should approach your parents. You never know, they could have a change of heart. It would be a lot better to be at home during your pregnancy. If not I can ask my Aunt Ellen if she knows of any places for single mothers. Even if she doesn't know of a place, there must be someone she can ask."

"Who is this Aunt Ellen? And why will she help me?"

"She is a pastor in charge of the youth ministry at her church. She is not the senior pastor, but she works with young people and would love to help."

"A pastor? You know I don't go to church, don't you?"

"That doesn't mean that she won't help you. This is what she has devoted her life to do."

"Not only that, she probably won't have too much to do just working with Christians."

"Not necessarily, Christians have their problems too." Ruth added.

"I feel a little better. Not great, but better. I can still go to school. I may have to slow down once the baby is here, but hopefully I won't have to stop completely."

"You'll cross that bridge when you get to it. Right now you have a simple game plan to start out with: one, get tested; next, talk to your parents, and Ruth will talk with Aunt Ellen. Shall we have more hot chocolate girls?" Shanice asked.

"Yes, why not, I mean it's only 2:00 in the morning! Why not stay up the whole night." Katy was being sarcastic again.

"Before we go to bed I think we should pray." Ruth said.

Katy rolled her eyes, "Ok, I don't suppose it'll hurt. It's better than a kick in the teeth."

Ruth began: "Dear Lord. Thank you for the end of another day, and the beginning of another. It is a day that you have made, and we will rejoice in it. Lord, I come boldly before your throne of grace, and present Katy and her unborn baby to you. You are the Lord God of all flesh and there is nothing too hard for you. I pray that you work things out for Katy, and that there will be no loss concerning her baby. I ask too Lord, that you go before her and smooth the way, but if there are any challenges, give Katy the grace to face them boldly. Father it is also my fervent prayer that my friends come to know you in a deeper way, and choose salvation and the path to life. These things I pray in Jesus' name. Amen."

"Ruth." Shanice said.

"Yes, Shanice." Ruth answered.

"I think I am ready to give my life to Christ."

And on that early morning in late November, Shanice said the prayer of salvation, also known as the sinner's prayer, and gave her life to Jesus.

CHAPTER 8

THE COLD, HARD TRUTH REVEALED

"See, I am sending you out like sheep among wolves. So be as cunning as serpents and as innocent as doves. " Matthew 10:16 (ISV)

The weeks were rolling by towards the end of the first semester, and Christmas. Everything ground to a standstill during this time because of exams: the girls had set certain goals for themselves, and they all wanted to take home an extra Christmas present of top grades to their families for the holidays.

Since accepting Christ, Shanice seemed more focused and less intent of craving attention. Ruth wondered whether the experience with Katy left her feeling that something similar could have happened to her. They never spoke about the fact that her so-called friends were planning on getting her a job at an escort service. Ruth could tell that this pained Shanice. As much as she was a bit giddy, and flirtatious with boys, Ruth would never have thought that she would go for anything like that. She wondered what it was about Shanice that her friends at uni had seen, to make them feel that she would have fallen for such an idea. No matter what, it was a total misreading of her personality. The whole adventure on the night of the party made her more reflective, and careful about falling headlong into peoples' friendship groups just because of the appearance of popularity.

Ruth was able to convince her to go to church with her a couple of times; she didn't want to force her to do anything against her will. It was a huge step for her, and Ruth knew that she would have to leave the Holy Spirit to carry out His work without interference from her.

Lizzy too seemed somewhat withdrawn. They still got together as much as they could for their meetings and catch-up sessions, but she said less and less. Both Ruth and Shanice felt that she had it in her mind to consummate the relationship with Brian, and knew that if she told them her plans they would both protest.

The girls got a better perspective of Lizzy's need to feel needed when she opened up a bit one day about the fact that her mum blamed her father's leaving on her. Apparently her dad wasn't ready to have babies because he wanted to continue studying after her parents married, but her mum really wanted to start a family. She became pregnant with Lizzy against the wishes of her father, and due to the cost of raising a new family as a young couple, he had to put aside his plans and find an additional job. Things never changed: he resented her mother, who thought that maybe having two more children would make him love her, but this had just the opposite effect, and he withdrew from his family altogether. He was there in body, but not much else, and when the girls were of a certain age, her parents divorced because he had begun seeing another woman. From what Lizzy said, he remarried, and was able to pursue his dream to get a PhD. His new wife had a son after he completed his studies.

Lizzy told them that as the first girl, she often played liaison officer between her parents, and she had to work out how best to get them talking and doing things as a family, and it made her a bit nervous seeing that she was never sure what mood either of them would be in. She desperately wanted her father to pay attention to her, but he only did when family or company visited: her parents' relationship was a complete sham to the outside world. When other people were around they were the happiest couple and family in the world, but behind closed doors they were two adult strangers and three needy girls living under the same roof. As a result of this, Lizzy loved food shopping because they had to go out as a family, her mum only learned to drive after her dad left, so they all piled into his car every Saturday morning, and had a great time shopping for food, and playing happy families. Anything that put them together under the scrutiny of others made her ecstatic!

Her account of her family cleared up her need for love and approval from an older man who was in some ways a father figure. The fact of the matter was that she just wanted to be validated as a person, and was transferring what she didn't receive as a child to her young adult life. Ruth at least got her to see Aunt Ellen on a regular basis. Lizzy needed professional help and she would give her friendly support at home, but leave the rest to someone who was certified to really help in a deeper, spiritual way. The only thing was that she didn't seem to want to stop seeing Brian. Ruth would just have to leave that to God.

One thing that Ruth and Shanice noticed was that Lizzy only seemed to go out with Brian on Friday nights, and occasionally for a coffee or a short date during the week. When they asked her why he couldn't see her on a Saturday or Sunday, she said that he used to weekend to grade, and prepare his lectures. They both found this a bit too regimented; never ever going out on the weekend with the person you supposedly loved? Something just didn't seem right.

Lizzy began talking about a special place that Brian was planning on taking her this coming Friday to mark the end of exams and the end of the term. He had already told her that he would be going away for all of the Christmas holidays. Where to? Ruth and Shanice wanted to know. Lizzy told them that he said that he had family in various parts of Europe and that he usually spent the holidays with them.

On Wednesday of the same week, Aunt Ellen called and asked whether she could speak to Lizzy. After the call, Lizzy told them that she was coming over to discuss some news with her, and wondered whether she would mind the girls being there, if not Lizzy could go to her office. Lizzy said that she didn't mind, and that she usually discussed things with the girls anyway. They prepared a tray of sandwiches and a pot of tea.

When Aunt Ellen arrived they realized that it began to snow: when they looked outside there was a blanket of white everywhere. They were glad that classes were over for the year and that they didn't have to venture out to classes the next morning, although they still had to go to work in the afternoon. Hopefully it would be melted by then, and the temperature would not plunge turning it to ice.

"Hello girls. How's everyone?" Aunt Ellen asked hugging and kissing them one at a time.

"Relieved that we have one semester behind us. It was a good term overall. And we've learned the tricks of the trade of survival in uni." Ruth said.

"Yes. I tell you Aunt Ellen. I want to do a master's degree, but am giving it some serious thought at the moment." Lizzy added.

"She's only saying that, Aunt Ellen. Lizzy is quite clever." Shanice said.

"Actually, thinking about it we aren't that bad are we girls?" Ruth said, and they looked at each other and began to laugh.

After having some sandwiches and tea, Aunt Ellen said "Well, I must say that the news I have is not going to put smiles on your faces, especially you Lizzy."

"It's about Professor Caledonia isn't it?" Shanice asked.

"Yes. It is, I'm afraid, Lizzy."

"What is it Aunt Ellen?" Lizzy asked in a whisper.

"Maybe you should see this." And she handed her a newspaper clipping.

Lizzy read it silently then she put it down on the sofa, and began to cry. Shanice took up the clipping and began to read. Ruth stood over her and read silently.

"Oh, the rat!" Shanice exclaimed. "How could he do this to the two of them? I knew he couldn't be trusted. Lizzy you are not still going out with him this Friday night are you?"

"Lizzy?" Ruth continued. "Are you still going to go out with him on Friday?"

"I don't know." Lizzy whispered.

"What do you mean you don't know? Haven't you read the clipping? He's married Lizzy, and is not separated from his wife. She's on a sabbatical in Germany assisting with research at the University of Berlin. There's the family he has all over Europe. He's just going to be with his wife and kid, Lizzy. You were just his bit on the side to keep him warm. How could you still consider wanting to see that man? If I were you I would call him now and cancel the date."

"Lizzy?" Aunt Ellen asked: "Is there a good reason you would still consider seeing this man?"

What Aunt Ellen had given Lizzy to read, was a clipping that she found in a paper a friend of hers had brought to her office earlier that week. There was an article about under-aged mail order brides that she wanted Aunt Ellen to see. After reading the article, Aunt Ellen was flipping through the rest of the paper, when she saw an article about a prominent young professor who was on sabbatical in Berlin from her University of London post. Her name was Dr Anita Caledonia and there was a picture with her and her husband, Professor Brian Caledonia, and their two-year old daughter, Danni. When asked how the young couple had been surviving being away from each other for the past eight months, she said that her husband spent every weekend with them, and that he would be in Berlin for a month over the Christmas break.

Lizzy felt sick, devastated really, but strangely enough she wanted to be with Brain at that very moment. She found herself in the middle again, just like when she was a child. She desperately wanted his love and approval, and even though at the back of her mind, she never dismissed the idea that he could have been lying to her about being still married to his wife, she just wanted the love of a father from him. Every action of hers cried out 'love me, please love me.'

"I'll go out with him and break it off at the end of the date."

"Lizzy, who are you fooling? Remember what Aunt Ellen said about intimacy? By the time he holds your hands, and begins stroking them while looking deeply into your eyes you won't even be thinking straight any more. How are you going to have the nerve to confront him with this news and more so, to break it off? You don't even know if he will turn on you." Shanice said.

"I think that he may think twice about becoming violent. He has too much to lose: his job, his marriage if it turns into a police affair. No, his type is too suave for violence. He'll somehow convince you that it was never meant to go this far, that he thinks that you are a nice girl, and that he couldn't help himself. By the end of the evening, you'll end up feeling sorry for him, and you'd be telling him that it's all right. You'll end up comforting him, and come home wondering what just happened. Then in a month's time he'll say that you could be friends, of course, this is just to keep you quiet, and keep you on a long leash. This is usually the M.O. of this type of sociopath. He is basically an insecure adult who preys on vulnerable younger, inexperienced young women with a huge void that needs filling." Aunt Ellen said. "Lizzy, my advice to you would be to call him and tell him that you are not going out with him this Friday, and during the break, begin to get accustomed to the fact that the relationship is over."

"I'll decide what to do tomorrow. Thanks Aunt Ellen." And with that she got up from the sofa and excused herself.

Needless to say, on Friday night Lizzy was as cheery as ever, singing Christmas songs while getting ready to go out with Brian. Shanice and Ruth did not know what to make of it. They both wondered whether she had mustered up the courage to face him in his lies, and break off the relationship. But how, and where? Would he bring her back home after a break up? But as Aunt Ellen said, part of his pathology was being a nice guy, so he wouldn't want to do anything to push Lizzy to do anything rash, therefore he would most probably offer to drive her home, open the door for her and kiss her on the cheek with a tear in his eye, making her feel guilty for leaving him. Ruth had spent quite a bit of time in prayer about the whole matter from the very beginning, and she knew that God was faithful, so while she looked on in mild apprehension as Lizzy got ready, she actually felt relieved about it, and knew in her heart that the end of the relationship was near, although she had no insight into how it would happen.

Lizzy looked smashing. She looked like a delicate flower in her emerald green knee-length chiffon dress. Her hair was done in a mess of curls à la Shirley Temple, her eyes were smoky charcoal, with a touch of silver, and her lips were shimmering with pale pink lip gloss. She was a picture of innocence, and Ruth hoped that she would return home with her innocence intact. Lizzy was somewhat of an enigma to her friends: she seemed bent on chasing happiness at the expense of her own happiness. Actually, Ruth sometimes wondered whether she even knew what happiness was, not theoretically, but experientially.

Lizzy was such a lovely girl, but a lot of her emotional intelligence consisted of a second-hand knowledge of things. She was following a script in her head based upon a combination of aspects of other people's lives, what she read in novels and thought seemed all right, and what she picked up from dramas on television. She was a shell of a person, and her choice of 'filling' was not always beneficial to her mental growth. What she really needed was a touch from Jesus, the gentle saviour who could take a person's mess and beautify it. Oh what a success it would be if her inner beauty could match her outward appearance of what the world deemed beautiful.

Ruth looked at her and knew in an instant why so many marriages ended in divorce. Looking at Lizzy with carnal eyes would be enough for so many men to want to be with her, overlook her spiritual flaws, because they themselves were flawed, and marry her. And as the relationship grew, or rather failed to grow, they would both believe that the only way to fix it, would be to move on in life, away from each other, and probably on to another hapless victim in the search for wholeness and completion. Ruth was on a personal crusade to get as many of her friends at uni saved as she could. She was not ashamed to talk about Jesus, and didn't mind the looks she received from the more cynical students on campus. Some listened to what she had to say out of good manners, but she didn't care, knowing that the planting of the seed was the most important thing. So far apart from Shanice, four other people became saved. What a victory! The angels were rejoicing.

When Brian arrived, he came upstairs to get Lizzy. He was dressed semi-casually, and looked smart. Lizzy warned both Ruth and Shanice not to say anything to him about what Aunt Ellen had shown them. She said that she would deal with it. Shanice was itching to let a hint drop, but decided to honour Lizzy's wish; she hoped that she didn't regret her decision to remain silent.

"So where are you two off to tonight?" Shanice asked.

"Oh, Brian is taking me to dinner then he has a surprise in store for me." Lizzy added quickly.

"A surprise? How exciting! Any hints at all Professor Caledonia?" Ruth and Shanice never stopped calling him by his professional title even though he had insisted they call him Brian several times.

"No girls. You can't pry it out of me. I am sure that after a romantic dinner on the twenty-fifth floor of the Glass Top Restaurant, Lizzy would be up for a surprise."

"I can't wait. Shall we go?" Lizzy was never comfortable with Brian and the girls together knowing how her friends felt about their relationship. And they left.

Ruth looked out the window to see them driving off, and prayed that she would be back safe, sound and ready to move on with her life without him. It was 7:30 pm.

CHAPTER 9

A DESPERATE CRY IN THE NIGHT

The fear of the LORD is the beginning of wisdom; all those who practice it have a good understanding. His praise endures forever! Psalm 111:10 (ESV)

Ruth shot up in bed! What time was it? And what was that noise? She felt for her mobile phone to see the time, then realised that it was ringing: that was the noise that woke her up. Who could be calling at 3:20 in the morning? Then her mind shot to Lizzy. She looked across towards her bed and could just barely see that it was empty. She turned on her reading lamp, and called out to Shanice before answering the phone.

"Shanice wake up. The phone's ringing. It may be Lizzy." Then she answered the phone.

"Hello? Hello? What? Lizzy? Stop crying? What's the matter?"

"Ruth. Ruth. Can you come get me? Please. I'm afraid."

By this time Shanice was sitting up in bed trying to piece together the conversation based on what Ruth was saying. "Where is she? And what's wrong with her?" she whispered.

"Just a minute Lizzy. Calm down. Where are you?" Pause. "Where? Ok, ok. I'll get my dad to come and get you. What?"

"No, please. Not your dad. Can't you get Aunt Ellen?" Lizzy snivelled.

"You just wait there. We'll be there as fast as we can. Don't worry. Try to calm down. Say a prayer. You have two on your phone that I sent you. Read them over and over until we come get you. Try not to worry. We'll be there. Maybe in an hour. Maybe shorter. Bye." Ruth began to dial her father.

As soon as the phone rang, Ruth's father picked it up. It was as if he was expecting a call. "Hello?" he said.

"Hello dad. We need your help dad. Lizzy is out with, erm, with her friend, and she seems to be in trouble. She called from the wash room. I think she is in a stall. The third one from the door on the left she said. Can you get me and we can go look for her dad?"

"Where exactly is she?"

"She said that she is at a club called Plato's Retreat in Soho. I'll check Google maps for the exact location dad."

"I'll call Ellen to stay with the kids and I'll come with your mum. We'll be there as soon as Ellen can get here. It shouldn't take her more than twenty minutes at this time of the morning. I'll call you when mum and I are downstairs. See you soon."

"Thanks. Bye dad. I love you."

"I love you too Ruth. Bye"

She turned to Shanice and said: "I wonder what happened to Brian?"

"Hm. But why is she in a toilet stall Ruth? Did she say why? I mean even if they had a fight and he left her, why is she in a toilet stall sounding so freaked out?"

"Yeah...I don't know Shanice. Have you ever heard of this club? Plato's Retreat? It's in Soho."

"Nope. Never heard of it. Shall we call her back and talk to her in the mean time?"

"In a minute. Let's check the location so I can give them to dad."

"Ok. I'll Google the club to see if it's a safe place. Although I can't see Professor Caledonia going to a sleazy joint even though he is a slime ball. I guess we should get dressed too huh?"

"I was wondering if you could stay here, Shanice. I mean, you never know. In her state of mind she could have decided to get a taxi and come home. If she does, somebody should be here to welcome her." Ruth said.

"All right." Then she let out a loud gasp. "Oh my good Lord!"

"What's the matter?" Ruth went to see what she was looking at on the computer. "Lord have mercy. No, no. How could she allow herself to get into that?" And they stared at each other.

"It says here that there is a lounge and bar at the front. Here. See, there's a picture of it. That other stuff is at the back." Shanice said.

"How could this happen to her? Do you think she was drinking and got a bit drunk?" Ruth asked.

"I guess that's the best explanation. Because as much as she likes the man, I don't think that Lizzy would go in for that business. She's too much of a private person."

Shanice Googled Plato's Retreat and found out that it was a sex club with a pretty normal-looking lounge and bar at the front, but from all appearances patrons of the club knew what they were going there for, and would not have thought that they just stumbled into the place innocently. What kind of person was Brian Caledonia? How could he think that their friend would want to get involved in such activities? It reminded Ruth of the temple orgies that the Bible spoke of. She felt really badly for Lizzy. She imagined that this would be the end of her relationship with Brian. What an ordeal!

It was quarter past four when her father and mother arrived at the flat. She had prepared a flask of tea, but neither one of them wanted any. She was glad to see her parents, but she did not know how she was going to tell them what kind of place Lizzy found herself in. There was a duvet on the seat next to her in the car.

"Hi mum and dad. How are you? Thanks for coming." She said.

"We're blessed Ruth dear. You know that mum looked up the club on the Internet so that I could plan the route." Her father said.

It was then that she realised that they probably knew what kind of place Plato's Retreat was. And...maybe that was why they had brought the duvet. Just in case Lizzy wasn't completely dressed. She hoped this was not the case. But one never knew.

"Oh. I see. Dad I'm sorry to drag you into this. We didn't know dad.

And Lizzy didn't know either. Her friend said that he had a surprise for her after dinner."

"That's awful. She's probably scared out of her wits. She's not that kind of girl is she? Don't those places have age limits? Dear Lord, what has the world come to?" Her mum said.

Her father remained silent. Ruth knew that he was angry. Not because Ruth called him to help, but because Brian would have taken her to a place like that. Dad was very protective of Ruth and her friends. She hoped that there wouldn't be a scene at the club.

They arrived there in about twenty minutes. Ruth was getting ready to get out of the car when her father said "Stay in the car Ruth. This is no place for young girls. Stay with mum."

"All right dad."

He took the duvet and went up to the front of the club and spoke with the bouncer. Ruth was sure that he would be able to enter the club and get Lizzy without a hassle. Dad could be very convincing when he was determined to get a thing done, and he was determined to bring Lizzy out of that den of iniquity in as little time as possible.

Mr Golden entered the club, and asked for the manager. When the man finally appeared, he told him that he had received a call on behalf of a scared patron and he had come to take her with him. The manager tried to tell him that nobody entered the club under duress, but Ruth's dad wasn't interested in hearing any stories. He just wanted him to go into the ladies wash room, ask the women there to step outside while he went inside and got Lizzy.

The manager looked aggravated to have had his evening disturbed by this man who didn't seem to want to listen to what he had to say, so he just did what he said. When they got to the wash room, the manager went inside and asked if all the women could step outside for a moment and Mr Golden went inside. On his way to the wash area, he kept his eyes peeled on the dimly lit walls not wanting to see any of the goings-on in the place. He kept pleading the Blood as he walked through the club.

When all the women were outside, he went inside and said "Lizzy. It's Ruth's dad, Mr Golden. I'm here to get you. Are you dressed?"

Lizzy stepped coyly out of the stall. She was fully dressed and didn't need the duvet. On the way out, she stopped to get her coat and they were soon in the car. Once inside, she began to cry uncontrollably. Mrs Golden went to the back seat, covered her with the duvet and hugged her all the way home. Lizzy was hysterical. When they got home, they all went up to the flat. Mr Golden sat in the living room, and Ruth's mum went into the bedroom with the girls. They stayed in there for almost an hour, then Ruth, Shanice and Mrs Golden came outside, and said that Lizzy was asleep.

"So who's this mysterious friend who seemed to have disappeared leaving a hysterical young woman in a place like that? Is he an older man? I really can't imagine a boy your age going to a place like that." Mr Golden asked.

Ruth and Shanice looked at each other. "Yes dad. Lizzy was seeing a professor from uni."

"A married one too." Shanice added.

"Dad, what can we do about it? I mean it was her choice, but we have been telling her to break it off since the beginning. Even Aunt Ellen was counselling her about it. And last week, she brought an article to show her that he wasn't separated from his wife as he had told her, but that his wife is actually in Germany doing research at the University of Berlin. They even have a two-year old."

"You see the only thing is that Lizzy is not a child. It was her choice to go with him after all. I can approach the university board and see if he can be dismissed or at least moved to another campus. As much as Lizzy had a say in the matter, he seemed to have preyed on her vulnerability. Professors aren't hired to date their students. It would have been different if he were single, and genuinely interested in having a relationship leading to marriage with her, but this was clearly not the case. I'll make a few calls and see how to proceed. I'll speak with you during the week. When will you be coming home Ruth?"

"Next Thursday. Thanks again mum and dad. God bless you."

"Thanks Uncle Frank, Aunt Pat." Shanice added.

"Call us if you need anything. What about Lizzy's mother. Is she in the city, or away?"

"She's in the city. We'll call her in the morning." Shanice said.

And with that Ruth's parents left. Shanice and Ruth made a pot of tea and sat on the sofa and chatted until the sun came up.

CHAPTER 10

CIRCLE OF FRIENDS

The fear of the LORD is the beginning of wisdom; all those who practice it have a good understanding. His praise endures forever! Psalm 111:10 (ESV)

*L*izzy finally woke up at one in the afternoon. She looked a mess, and Ruth and Shanice had the feeling that she was hung over. She went to the bathroom and took a shower, then they all went into the kitchen to eat. Lizzy was crying silently, and the girls cuddled her in a group hug.

"What would I have done if your dad hadn't come Ruth?"

"Well that was not going to happen, and you are here safe and sound now. What happened Lizzy?"

"Well, the night started out really well. We went to a brill restaurant on the twenty-fifth floor of a building overlooking the river. We had champagne, two bottles. As a matter of fact I think I had most of it. I was trying to build up my courage to tell Brian that I knew that he was not separated from his wife, but I really overdid it with the alcohol."

Shanice and Ruth remained silent. Neither one of them thought that this was an appropriate time for "I told you so."

Lizzy went on speaking: "When we left the restaurant he asked me if I wanted to go back to his place and I said yes. I was a bit tired and really wanted a cup of coffee before continuing on with the evening."

Ruth and Shanice looked at each other. They both hoped that coffee was all they had at Brian's place.

"We got to his place at around one, and spent a bit of time there, chatting, and cuddling a bit."

"Why would you want to cuddle with somebody you were planning on breaking up with? Lizzy please don't tell me that you did more than cuddling. Remember what Aunt Ellen said about it being almost impossible to wrangle yourself out of a situation once a certain stage is arrived at. Look, did you or didn't you?" Shanice wanted her to get to the point of the story.

"I didn't."

"How come?" Shanice asked. She didn't believe her.

"Because Brian kept telling me just how special the rest of the night would be, and that he wanted me to be ready for it. Anyway we left his place and headed for the club, and at first it was fine. We stayed in the lounge for about an hour, I'm not sure any more, but I do know that he ordered another bottle of champagne and I carried on drinking."

"So when were you planning on breaking it off with him, Lizzy?" Ruth asked. She didn't want to interrupt, but nothing Lizzy said so far convinced her that she wanted to end her relationship with Brian. If she really did want to, she would have done it over dinner. She would not have ended up at his house almost compromising her position with him. Nor would she have had the opportunity to end up at that disgusting club. What was Lizzy thinking? She really needed help. But hopefully she had seen the light after what ended up happening.

"Well, once I started drinking it got harder and harder to say anything. I started thinking that maybe I would text him while he was away."

"And then what? Are you saying that you would have been able to sit in another of his lectures without feeling anything for him? And I am sure he would have wanted to get together to 'discuss' the break up." Shanice said.

"Look. I don't know right. I messed up. I know I messed up. You don't have to rub it in, ok?" Lizzy started sounding hysterical again.

"Anyway, after spending some time in the lounge Brian asked me whether I was ready to go on through to the back. I said yes, because I thought that maybe it was dancing or something. So he told me to follow a hostess, and that he would join me on the main floor in about ten minutes. I said ok, and got up and followed a woman to the back of the club, and then was when I saw what was happening. I had never seen anything like it in my life, and I felt really sick. I wanted to throw up. I was so scared. I knew that I had to think fast, so I told the hostess that I wanted to use the toilet and it was then that I called you."

"So you don't know what happened to Brian? Did he leave?"

"No, he didn't leave. When I was leaving the club with your dad I saw him in the main hall with someone else. He had totally forgotten about me. He didn't even see me leaving." She began to cry again.

"So...what's next Lizzy? This is not just some teenage crush that you are embarrassed about. This man, this married man tried to humiliate you in the most disgusting way in public with a bunch of strangers. You could have caught something there. I mean, do they even do any health checks? Not only that, did you consider that someone could have taken your picture, and you could have ended up on You Tube or Facebook, or some X-rated Internet site in flagrante delicto? Do you know that Ruth's dad is going to the university board to see if he can get Caledonia sacked or moved to another campus?" After she said it, Shanice wasn't sure whether she was supposed to have said anything. But it was too late now so she quickly added: "Please don't text him and warn him. I hope you realise just how serious this is."

"Yes. I do. I feel terrible. But now I know who he really is, and that he never really cared about me in the first place." Ruth and Shanice breathed a sigh of relief. At last Lizzy saw the light. "I am so glad that the term is over, so I won't have to see him, hopefully never again. I am definitely not taking his second semester course. Oh! How could I have been so stupid? You tried to warn me, but I thought that I knew better. I feel really lucky that I was at least sober enough to realise what was going on. I can imagine that if I had had more to drink he could have taken advantage of me. Ruth, what do your parents think of me? They must think that I am no good at all. How embarrassing!"

"Of course they don't think that. You got yourself into a bit of trouble, and you reached out for help. That is the action of someone who didn't want to be in that situation. You didn't stay and come back home after a night of debauchery, you chose to leave. So that says a lot."

"Thanks Ruth, you always know how to make a person feel good. Does Aunt Ellen know?"

"Mum and dad probably filled her in. She is going to think that I wasted our counselling sessions, isn't she?"

"You know Lizzy; the truth of the matter is that you need to be born again to be truly helped. Christian counselling is not psychiatry which depends on the will of an individual to produce results. In many cases people relapse into old habits with that kind of treatment, or they need to take drugs, or medication over long periods. These drugs sometimes alter their chemical imbalance in certain areas. I don't know too much about it, but that's what I've heard. A Christian counsellor receives guidance from the Holy Spirit who guides us into all truth. There is a very interesting passage in the Bible that tells us that we wrestle not against flesh and blood, but against principalities, powers and rulers of wickedness in high places."

"What does that mean?" Lizzy wanted to know.

"Yeah. I'm confuffled with that one too Ruth. What's all this principalities and powers business about?"

"Ok, you know that Satan is a spirit, righ?"

"Yes. That we know. Like God, God is spirit too, right?"

"Right. Can you see a spirit?" Ruth asked.

"Well in the horror movies you sometimes can. But not ghosts." Shanice added.

"Well, Hollywood movies are probably not the best guide to go by, but the bottom line is that we can't see spirits, but they are there."

"How do we know?" Lizzy.

"What type of fruit do you get from an apple tree? "Ruth asked.

"Apples, of course. What does this have to do with the conversation Ruth?" Lizzy sounded confused.

"Don't worry, I'm going somewhere with this, trust me. And what sort of fruit do you get from an orange tree?"

"Oranges." Shanice said.

"Good. We are clear on that. Do you remember back in secondary school on the way to the bus, there used to be a man who acted crazy and you used to say that he was possessed?" Ruth asked.

"Oh, ha ha ha. I remember that weirdo. Oh he was possessed all right." Lizzy said.

"What made you say that?" Ruth pressed her.

"Well for one he was always talking to himself out loud, and he used to swear at that woman's dog, remember?"

"And don't forget that he used to pull out his hair and talk to it. That freaked me out big time." Shanice said.

"So then, if I said to you that he was a tree." Lizzy and Shanice looked at each other. Ruth continued, "What kind of fruit did he bear?"

There was a brief silence, and then Lizzy shouted, "I see. I get it, I get it. I think his tree bore the fruit of madness, weirdness and hate and some others too."

"Perfect. Would you say that the three of us love each other?" Ruth asked.

"Yes, of course we do."

"How do you know?"

"Well, we care for each other, we show kindness and gentleness and we try to be nice to each other." Shanice added.

"So these are the fruit of our tree of love. Well these actions come from a spirit that makes us behave the way we do. We can't see the spirit, but we see the results of them. The mad man produced evil fruit and we saw them, we as friends showing love produce loving fruit and we see them too."

"So Lizzy, the problems you are having can't be helped by just talking about them, they are the only fruit you know how to produce as a result of everything in your life that has ever hurt you or robbed you of joy and happiness. All spirits need bodies to live in, and when a person is not filled with the Holy Spirit of God, other spirits enter and produce the fruit that they represent. When you are saved God works in you shaping you into the image of Jesus and you begin to produce good fruit. So my friend, although you understand what I am saying to you intellectually, you need to be saved for the benefits of salvation to be added to you. There is nothing more that I can tell you than that. All the chats and counselling with Aunt Ellen won't change a thing."

"I know. I will think about it. I really feel that I want to be saved after what happened."

"So, what's stopping you?" Shanice asked.

"I don't know. I don't know."

"Satan, the prince of this world has clouded your judgement. Satan is the father of all lies, Lizzy, he is a master seducer. He pretends to be an angel of light, that's what his name, Lucifer, means, but he is nothing more than a liar and a deceiver. He doesn't love people, especially if you are saved. The Bible tells us that he comes to steal, kill and destroy. Think of what happened to you last night. Can you point out what benefits at all there were to that experience?"

"Well, the dinner was lovely. That was so good, even you would have enjoyed it Ruth, you too Shanice."

"And what else. What about the after effects of the alcohol. Was that of any benefit to you?" Ruth asked.

"No, I wouldn't say that. I still feel sick, and woozy. I can't even move my head fast without it spinning."

"And then there was Brian's house. Any benefits there?"

"Not really. I suppose the cuddling was nice." And she blushed.

"I think we've been over this before. Aunt Ellen explained. The world tells us that it is ok to be intimate with someone that you are not married to, but it isn't. If you check the statistics for STDs, unwanted pregnancies, broken hearts and relationships, rapes and the list goes on, you can usually trace them to people who crossed a boundary that God clearly forbids in His word. God is and always will be God, and He is supreme. No matter what the telly, magazines, the radio and the government say, you cannot break God's laws and not pay the penalty for doing so. And that goes for Christians too by the way."

"So what about married people who are not saved?"

"What about them?" Ruth asked.

"Well, you are saying that God's laws shouldn't be broken, but what if you have an unsaved couple who decided to wait before sleeping together, then get married?"

"Well, great that they did not commit fornication, but there are other aspects of life that we have to consider too. It's not all about sex. Are they truthful, do they steal, cheat, blaspheme, live clean lives? Are they kind to their neighbours or are they selfish and greedy? You see what I mean. Life is a composite, isn't it? I think that we focussed mostly on fornication in our discussions with Aunt Ellen because you guys had questions about relationships, but there is a whole lot more to life than sex. Take uni for example. Would you cheat on an exam? Or, would you plagiarise an essay?"

"No! Of course not. That is wrong!"

"Ah, you see. That *is* wrong. That's what I mean about life. There's a lot more to it isn't there?" Ruth said.

"But it seems so hard. There are so many rules if you are a Christian. I don't know if I could live up to those standards. Maybe that's why I want to wait. I want to live a little first." Lizzy explained.

"You know what the truth is? There are only two laws that we have to live by." Ruth said.

"What? Only two? I must admit Ruthie; it seems like a whole lot more." Shanice said. "Can you explain how come there are only two?"

"Ok. Where shall I start? In the Old Testament there were the Ten Commandments. You've both heard about those, we had them in RE."

"How could we ever forget?" Shanice chimed in.

"Well, now there are only two. And the beauty of it is that when you obey those two, you obey all the rest." Ruth added confidently.

"Wow! So, what are these two laws? I can't wait to hear this. Are you sure Ruth?"

Ruth smiled: "I am as sure as the nose on my face. The first law says that we should love God."

"And what's the next one?"

"That we should love our neighbour as we love ourselves."

"Wait a minute. I thought you said that if you follow those two, you follow all the rest. I remember from RE class one saying not to steal and another not to covet things from your neighbour. What do they have to do with love?"

"Ok. Let's use ourselves. You know how you admire Annette's sports car from flat 3C? Would you steal it?"

"Of course not! You know that." Lizzy said.

"Why not?" Shanice asked.

"That's easy: it's wrong to steal."

"Yes. But why?"

"Well, you could go to jail."

"So are you saying that the only reason why you wouldn't steal her car is that you don't want to go to prison? What if you could steal it, and never be caught? Would you do it?"

"Never. I am not a thief. End of matter." Lizzy was adamant.

"Right. Good. I want you to think about why you would never steal. And don't say that your mum told you not to. That's just like the not going to prison reason."

"Ok. Let's see. Why wouldn't I steal? Well I suppose that she worked hard for her own money to buy something that she wanted, and if I took it from her, I would be inconveniencing her. I mean, she would be upset, and would suffer a loss because if the car was never found then even if she got back money from her insurance, she would still be without that thing that she loved, or cherished."

"Ah. Now you've got it. So you wouldn't steal because you loved your neighbour."

"Well I don't love her. But I know what you mean."

"The love we are talking about here is the God kind of love. Hold on I want to read one of my favourite Bible verses to you. I particularly like it from the Amplified Bible. Here, it says: 'Love endures long and is patient and kind; love never is envious nor boils over with jealousy, is not boastful or vainglorious, does not display itself haughtily. It is not conceited (arrogant and inflated with pride); it is not rude (unmannerly) and does not act unbecomingly. Love (God's love in us) does not insist on its own rights or its own way, for it is not self-seeking; it is not touchy or fretful or resentful; it takes no account of the evil done to it [it pays no attention to a suffered wrong]. It does not rejoice at injustice and

86

unrighteousness, but rejoices when right and truth prevail. Love bears up under anything and everything that comes, is ever ready to believe the best of every person, its hopes are fadeless under all circumstances, and it endures everything [without weakening]. Love never fails [never fades out or becomes obsolete or comes to an end].' Is that the most beautiful thing you have ever heard? How could anybody ever think of hurting another person if they kept that in mind? I have to read it every day to help me to overcome certain challenges."

"What challenges do you have, Ruth?" Shanice wanted to know.

"Oh I have a few. You would be surprised." And she giggled.

"But what about someone like Aunt Ellen who lived her life and is now a Pastor is she going to be taken to task by God?" Lizzy asked.

"Well, first of all when we become saved and accept Jesus as our Lord we become part of God's family, and we are in the body of Christ. The blood of Jesus is a powerful weapon and when God sees us, He only sees Jesus' blood that was shed on the cross. The Bible says that there is no condemnation for those who are in Christ. But that doesn't mean that we could just decide to sin over and over again, and not suffer some consequences. We are sinners by nature, but the grace of God in our lives kind of makes us want to live in a certain way."

Ruth continued: "What you also need to remember is some of the things Aunt Ellen said about her life when she was living without God. She was isolated from her family, she had a nervous breakdown, and she felt a lot of emptiness. Remember she also said that with all the alcohol, cigarettes friends and partying, at the end of the day, she still wanted something more. These are some of the side effects of a life without God."

"We get it. That's deep stuff."

"But what if I never meet anybody who loves me?" Lizzy asked. "I just wanted Brian to love me. Just as I wanted my dad to love me."

"Faith my friend. Remember what we said about faith? Why do you think that God would want you to live a life without love? Not only that, with salvation you have a new family of people who are in Christ and who love and care about you. Also, when you are really living for God you never know whether you would choose to want to serve him as a single person. There is such a fulfillment that comes with devoting your life to God that this may be the way you end up."

"What? No way!" Lizzy shouted.

"Look, all I am trying to say is that we have to leave ourselves open to the leading of the Holy Spirit in our lives. And know that we are given grace and strength to endure whatever state we end up in: single or married. God gives you that assurance, that His grace is sufficient for all of us."

"While that's all true, right now, I say we have lunch. It's four o'clock." Shanice decided that this was a good juncture to end the conversation.

The girls got up and began to prepare lunch while Lizzy went to lie on the sofa.

CHAPTER 11

CHRISTMAS IS LOVE

An Advent Prayer

Father God, thank you for each family member is this season. Teach us to honor you and love others, especially those who seem hardest to love. Help us to appreciate and celebrate each other's uniqueness and differences, and help us especially not to try and fit others into our personal molds. You made our families, and by wisdom, placed each person in their families. Thank you for loving us, and teaching us how to love others. In Jesus' name. Amen

Four days before Christmas, Ruth, Lizzy and Shanice had their last dinner together before leaving the flat to go home for the holidays. Ruth's dad took both Lizzy and Shanice home before continuing on to their home in north London. It was a bitter-sweet experience saying goodbye to their flat. The girls had grown a lot since September when they left their parents' homes to venture out on their own. On their last night together after dinner they exchanged gifts, and had a long chat about the semester: its ups and downs. Amidst laughter and tears they remembered some of the more memorable events of the past four months. The all decided that the highlight of the term was the fact that they became closer as friends, and that they had never once had a falling out. Although they did not always agree on everything, they managed to negotiate their way through each hurdle and challenge. Lizzy and Shanice both thought that if it were not for Ruth and her wisdom they may have had a few quarrels.

Shanice was not particularly excited about going home too much anymore because her older brother had been sent to prison, and she knew that her mother would not be full of seasonal cheer for the next three weeks. Ruth told her that she would love to have her, if ever things became too much for her to bear, but she reminded her that she should be there for her mother to give her support, and minister to her when she needed comforting. She reminded her that she was now a member of God's family, and so His grace would always be sufficient for her in all situations. Ruth had bought them both Bibles along with their Christmas presents, and asked that they try to read a little each day. She said that the Psalms were probably a good place to start, and gave them a few of her favourite ones.

When Ruth's dad dropped them off, they hugged each other for a long time, not wanting to release their hold on each other. It was an emotional time. On the drive home her father said: "You know Ruth, I am quite proud of you. I mean more than I was before. When you first told us that you were planning on leaving, it was difficult to imagine. The night after we had our discussion over dinner mother and I prayed, and she had a revelation as to why you wanted to leave. You may have noticed that I did not press you too much after our initial chat. I was just a bit concerned that your friends seemed to have had the better deal in terms of your study arrangements. But afterwards mum reminded me that God was in charge. Your mother's revelation was that you only wanted to move out to be the glue that held your friends' lives together. This was extremely selfless and loving of you. Your talk of our being too strict was just a seemingly appropriate excuse you used to get your argument for leaving across. You are a fine young lady, and we are really very proud of how you handled yourself over the past few months. You never once forgot who you are in Christ. You were a blessing to your friends, and also to their friends."

"Thanks dad. I wondered which one of you would catch the revelation. I must admit that you were rather calm after our talk. I only did exactly what you and mum would have done. You are great parents."

"So have you decided whether you will be moving back home for the next school year?"

"I actually thought about it back in September when I really felt the pressure of working and going to uni. But I can't say right now dad. Home is that best place that I have ever been. There's no disputing that. But I'll have to wait and see. I love you dad."

"I love you too Ruth."

They drove in silence the rest of the way. The traffic was relatively clear for this time of year, so they were home in forty minutes.

When Ruth entered the front door John and Hannah rushed to meet her. She was so glad to see them. Although only a few months had passed they both seemed to have grown.

"Hello Ruthie. We've been waiting ages for you to get back. What took you so long anyway? Was daddy driving like grandpa again?" Jonathan asked.

"No John. He actually drove like grandma this time." Ruth said and they all laughed.

"Remind me to have you use public transport next time." Their father joked.

"Where's mum? Mum? Mummy?" Ruth walked through the hall and towards the living room looking for her mother.

"Mum just stepped out to get a few things for dinner. We are having all your favourites Ruthie." Hannah said. "It smells so good in here. Can I help with your things?"

"No thank you young lady. I know what you want to get up to. No snooping around in my bags to peek at presents. I haven't got you anything anyway." And Ruth tickled Hannah.

"You wouldn't dare, would you? Dad, Ruth said she didn't get me anything. Can she do that dad?" Hannah went looking for their father who was taking Ruth's bags up to her room.

"Yes she can, and so can mum and I. No presents for Hannah this year."

"Daddy! Stop that."

"Ha ha! Serves you right." Jonathan teased.

"Don't think there's anything for you either young man." Ruth said to her brother.

She went up to her room to freshen up then came back downstairs. By the time she had done that her mother was back.

"Hi mum. Oh, I couldn't wait to see you. Want some help?"

"Not really but you can do some peeling for me if you insist." They all piled into the kitchen and either helped their mother or sat round listening to Ruth's funny stories about university.

"Ruth," Jonathan said, "Hannah said that when she goes to uni, she wants to move out with her friends too."

"Oh no you don't young lady." Ruth said. "I strictly forbid it."

"You can't do that. You're not my mother. If you did it why can't I? Eh dad?"

"Listen to you big sister, Hannah. She knows more about it than any of us, and if she says no, then she must know what she's talking about." Her father said.

"So Ruth," Jonathan said again, "Do you have a boyfriend?"

"No Jonathan. And you shouldn't be asking such questions."

"Why not?" Hannah wanted to know. "When I am older, I'm going to have a boyfriend."

"You'll have a lot of time for that yet. I can't believe you talking about boyfriends at age eight."

"But my friend Mandy has a boyfriend, and she's in my class. She says that they are going to get married someday."

"Isn't she the same one who wanted to run away and join a circus last year? And they all laughed.

Dinner was ready and they all chipped in to set the dining room table. The table was a vision for sore eyes and hungry bellies. And the smell was a delight. Mum had outdone herself this time. What a beautiful scene. Ruth took a picture of the table with all the food, and another one of her family standing around. When all the preparations were done they held hands and said a prayer of thanksgiving. It was truly a joyous occasion. Ruth wondered what her mother was going to prepare for Christmas if this was what she laid out three days before the holiday.

"Wow, mum. What are you planning on making for Christmas? I can't imagine that there is too much else left for you to cook." Ruth said.

"Well, that is precisely why we are celebrating like this tonight." Her father said.

"I don't understand. What do you mean?"

"Yeah dad. Why did you say that?" Jonathan asked.

"Shall we tell them now Pat?" Their father asked.

"Tell us what you guys? Did I miss something?" Hannah asked.

"You didn't Hannah dear. We haven't revealed anything yet."

"Mum...dad. What's going on?" Ruth asked.

"Well we have a little surprise for you all."

"A surpise? What, what? Are we going to Euro Disney? Oh mum. Please say yes." Hannah said impatiently.

"No, I'm afraid not. We are spending the next three days in Brixton."

"Brixton? Why Brixton?" Ruth wanted to know. "And why are we spending my birthday away from home. You do remember that my birthday is on the 26th of December, don't you?"

"Oh yes we do, who could ever forget that you are a Boxing Day baby." Jonathan joked. "I am sure mum and dad thought of giving you away when they saw you."

"Very funny John. It's not too late to give you away to the bin men you know." And Ruth stuck her tongue out at him.

"Enough of that you two." Dad said. "We have had this invitation for almost nineteen years now, and it is an obligation that we vowed to fulfil. I'm afraid that I can't say anything more right now."

"Mum, can you say any more?"

"Sorry my dears. You'll just have to be patient about this one. After dinner just pack a few things for the trip. We'll only be gone for two days and a bit. We are aiming to leave on Christmas Eve at around 5:00 o'clock."

"Oh...and one more thing. Aunt Ellen will be coming with us."

"Yay! Aunt Ellen. Cool!" Hannah squealed.

They all looked at her and laughed. Ruth went to the stereo player and put on some Christmas music, and they continued eating dinner laughing and chatting through it all. Ruth's mind was working overtime wondering what the big surprise was about. She loved a mystery and she tried to unravel all the possible reasons why her parents would choose to accept a nineteen year old invitation to Brixton over this particular Christmas. And, in addition to this, why would Aunt Ellen be coming along? Hm, it seemed like a surprise to top all surprises. But, she would just have to wait for it all to come to pass to know what the secret behind it was. She did intend, however, to try to pry bits and pieces out of her mother over the next day. She knew that her father would not budge, but she might just get a little out of mum.

CHAPTER 12

WHO IS RUTH?

At that time Mary got ready and hurried to a town in the hill country of Judea, where she entered Zechariah's home and greeted Elizabeth. When Elizabeth heard Mary's greeting, the baby leaped in her womb, and Elizabeth was filled with the Holy Spirit. In a loud voice she exclaimed: "Blessed are you among women, and blessed is the child you will bear! Luke 1:39-42 (NIV)

The drive to Brixton was like an endless game of Twenty Questions. The children bombarded their parents and Aunt Ellen with all manner of questions regarding where they were going. All they could ascertain from the barrage of who, why, where, and whats, was that they were going to the house of a woman. As to whom she was, what she did, why a nineteen year old invitation, they got no satisfaction.

At one stage Hannah with her wild and active imagination began to make up a story. Mother, who always encouraged her to write, told her to take out her jotter and begin writing her story, and she did. This kept her quiet for a good chunk of the journey.

Jonathan was sure that he had cracked the mystery. He said that they were going to visit a long, lost rich relative who was going to die, and leave them all her wealth. As to how come she had issued the invitation nineteen years earlier, he was unable to explain and he too set about to fine tune the end of his version of things.

Ruth was also questioning, but she had begun to wonder how come the invitation seemed to coincide with her birthday, but not only her birthday, but her nineteenth birthday. A nineteen year old invitation and her nineteenth birthday: was there some connection? Or was this just a coincidence. She had heard Pastor Richard say so many times that there are no coincidences, but God incidences, that she began to wonder what the link in events was. She asked her parents: "Mum, dad how come this invitation seems to coincide with my birthday? I mean if it were an eighteen year old invitation then it would be different. No. Wait. Actually, any age of the invitation would coincide with my birthday. Hey. What is this? Does this have to do with me? No, that couldn't be possible. I mean, who is this woman and why would she want to see me on my nineteenth birthday anyway. Nah. That's not it. This has nothing to do with me. Sorry Pastor Richard. There are coincidences in life after all." Ruth didn't see her parents look at each other. Then she too sank into silence thinking more about the soon to be revealed secret.

Aunt Ellen didn't say too much during the journey. She sat reading her Bible, and when Ruth looked to see what she was reading she saw that it was the first chapter of the book of Luke, about the pregnancy of Elizabeth and Mary. She seemed to be focussed on just that chapter.

The traffic was very heavy and they took over two hours to get there. By the time they pulled up outside a dimly-lit house it was almost eight o'clock. Dad went to the door and rang the bell while the rest of the family got their things out of the boot of the car. It was a cold, clear night. Ruth had to adjust her scarf and button up the top of her coat. When they got their things and locked up the car they joined dad at the top of the steps. It had been about a minute since he rang the bell, but nobody came to the door. After a while, they heard a shuffling inside, and the lock turning. The door opened and a woman stood in front of them.

At first glance in the hallway light she looked very familiar to Ruth and she wondered where she had seen her before. "Welcome." She said to them. "Pat, Frank it is truly a good thing to see you again after all this time. The years have flown." The stranger spoke slowly and measured her words. Her voice was deep and husky, and by the sound of her intonation she sounded West Indian, but Ruth wasn't sure. She knew that there was something distinctly foreign about her.

"Do come in all of you. I am sure that the traffic was a nightmare, and it is freezing tonight. I have a fire burning." They all went inside after the woman, and she led them into a large living room with a roaring fire. It was nice and warm in the room.

"Please let me take your things. Take your coats off and have a seat. Do. I'll have Martha make some hot chocolate." And she left the room.

They all sat on the plush, overstuffed sofas. Hannah hugged a cushion and sighed. "Oh mum, these are lovely. I want some of these for my bed." The woman re-entered the living room and turned on more lights. Ruth had a better look at her, and still got the distinct feeling that she had seen this woman some place before. She hated it when something like this nagged her. She wondered whether she should ask if she was a television presenter, but thought that she would just wait and find out who she was and what she did. As the lights brightened the room Hannah looked at the stranger and blurted out:

"Wow! You look just like Ruthie. Look Ruthie, do you see? She looks like you."

And it was then that Ruth realised why this woman seemed so familiar, Ruth saw her every day, each time she looked in the mirror. Hannah was right, she looked uncannily like her. She stared intently at the stranger who was smiling at her, and felt a warm glow of recognition. At that precise moment she heard the words 'this is your mother' echoing in her soul. It was the most primal experience she had ever had, but she knew that it was the truth.

"Ellen, maybe you can you take Hannah and Jonathan upstairs and show them their rooms. Martha will show you where they are." And they left with Aunt Ellen.

"Are you my mother?" Ruth asked softly when they left the room. "I mean, are you my birth mother. I look just like you."

"Yes Ruth, I am the woman who gave birth to you almost nineteen years ago."

"Mum, dad? What's going on? How come? I never knew. I never suspected."

"How could you have my dear? You are, and have always been loved. My name is Angelique Ruth Hayforth. Come over here let me show you something." She beckoned to Ruth as she made her way to a mantelpiece at the other end of the room. She opened the top draw and took out a larger album with the word 'Ruth' on the cover. "Have a look inside." She said to Ruth.

Ruth opened the album and turned the pages slowly. Tears rolled down her cheeks. On page after page there were photographs of her as a baby, toddler and through all the stages of her development. But not only were there pictures, but photocopies of her school reports, all her achievements, and just about everything that mum and dad had collect over the years to do with her. The album with filled with loving memories of the child she gave up when she was just a young girl a little younger than Ruth.

Angelique Ruth Hayforth had been sent to London to live with a great aunt fleeing an abusive uncle who had taken her parents in after a devastating hurricane. Unfortunately, as repayment for his bread and board, he turned his attention on the young Angelique. When she came to London, she realised that she was pregnant, and her great aunt made her give her baby up for adoption not wanting to be saddled with two more mouths to feed. The one thing that she asked Ruth's adoptive parents was that she be sent pictures of her baby, and that she had the opportunity to meet her on her nineteenth birthday. Pat and Frank Golden went one step further and sent updates of every achievement of her daughter throughout the years. And now here she was meeting her two days before her nineteenth birthday.

Ruth was in floods of tears and her mother, Pat went and sat next to her on the sofa comforting her. "Why are you crying Ruth? Tell me; are these tears of sadness or joy?"

"Oh mum. I feel so very fortunate to have been loved so much by so many people. Why do people who are adopted feel so angry when they should feel the joy of having been wanted by someone? Even if their parents did not want them out of the ignorance of the love of God, at least they had the wisdom to give them to someone who cared. That in itself is such an act of love. It is an unselfish act of love. It is not an act of hatred on the part of their mother or parents, but a pure act of selfless love. And you mum and dad, and you Miss Angelique my birth mother have all proven that you had nothing but love for me. This is the best Christmas and birthday gift that I could have ever hoped for. Thank you God, and thank you all." And she hugged her mother and wept.

When she stopped crying, she got up and approached Angelique. "We have not officially been introduced; my name is Ruth Angelique Golden. Mother I am ever so glad to meet you." And she hugged her long and hard. "I love you." She whispered in her ear.

Aunt Ellen entered just as she was hugging Angelique. "Is everything all right?" she asked.

"Yes, it is. It went very smoothly." Ruth's father answered.

"I never had an ounce of doubt that it wouldn't. Ruth is a very balanced young woman. She has been raised and taught well. The love of God resides solidly in her, and she has wisdom beyond her years. I did as you asked and spoke with Hannah and Jonathan. They had a lot of questions but they handled the information well. They will have more questions of course, but they will have all their answers in due time. They are in the kitchen with Martha enjoying her hot chocolate and gingerbread cookies."

"Good, shall we join them?" Angelique said. "We have a feast waiting. I hope you are all very hungry."

"I most certainly am famished. All this love has given me an appetite." Ruth smiled contentedly as she said it.

They went into the kitchen; Ruth walked between her mother and Angelique, hugging them both around the waist.

THE END